HATE IS NO SOLUTION

Jean Pailler

To those whose friendship has helped me to embark on this project

Ricky, Dave, and more…

FOREWORD TO THIS EDITION

Stephen Yaxley-Lennon, the charismatic young leader of a group of British patriots, also known as Tommy Robinson, seems to be in trouble again. He does not seem to come to terms easily with the police, and many people think he is having a raw deal and is being persecuted. I know nothing about persecution, but I do think he is being treated with unusual and unfair harshness.

I am I no position to speak against the administration of justice in the United Kingdom. Not out of fear but because I lack precise information. It seems, however, that Mr Yaxley-Lennon has been submitted to police proceedings that were not supported by any court ruling, and disproportionate with the threat he could represent to law and order.

I believe, indeed that any restriction to Mr Yaxley-Lennon's right of expression, freedom of thought and of speech, is counterproductive and could only result in him and his friends taking a stronger stand, to the risk of breaking the peace.

As an enthusiastic friend of British culture, I feel this situation very distressing, In this very special year of 2015, eight centuries exactly after the Magna Carta was given as the first example of balancing rights and powers,

I have signed, a few days ago, a petition circulated in the public, and directed to the Prime Minister, the Honourable David Cameron, MP, asking him to order an independent review into the treatment of Stephen Yaxley-Lennon. This third edition of my book comes as a confirmation of my signature. I publish it as an act of solidarity with Mr Yaxley-Lennon. I am far from sharing his opinions, far indeed from seeing a certainly difficult situation from the same angle. Should my support, however, be considered as improper, offensive, or breaking any rule of law, I would take my full responsibility and readily answer for my actions before a British court.

September, 2015

FOREWORD

TO THE SECOND EDITION

This unpretentious book – rather a note-book - gathers my impressions and reflexions along a few weeks on an issue that is very important and very grave, the shallow product of my observation of differences that are very deep-rooted.

As I was "blogging" and writing, I had a dialogue with virtual correspondents on the internet, through social networks as Facebook and Twitter. It was quite an experience. Talking rough and trading insults is quite easy on these media. In fact it is part of the game, and I feel no shame in admitting that I engage in it often gleefully. Actually, it is a very useful means of screening and sifting one's interlocutors. After a few tweets exchanged, one can tell anger from venomous hate and humorous banter from loudmouth stupidity, as well as recognise those "star-twitters" who never have the courtesy to answer a message from someone whom they have not been properly introduced to. One does tire easily of the Misses Foxgloves, Brawny Bills and SuperMo's of the Sphere (this does not allude to any individual account and must not be taken personally). I had the good fortune, however, to meet a few users of the network, who were willing to talk and to exchange ideas.

Dialogue usually started with a strong opposition; then - mutual good faith once admitted – each listened to the other's message and, even if we did not come to terms, each of us understood the legitimacy of the other's reasoning. I believe no conversation can take place when any of the people concerned writes off as "bullshit" another's line of arguing. It takes two to make a fight – it takes two also to come to an agreement. Mutual respect, tolerance, and an effort to understand the other's point of view are essential. And I must say that I have found them in this somewhat difficult exchange of ideas.

Respect, however, is not submission. No more than tolerance is compromise. From reactions received after the first edition, I have had to admit that, out of a desire of appeasing the dialogue, I had perhaps given the impression that I was ready to concede on major issues. This I am not.

Our European civilisation is founded on Freedom. Freedom of will, freedom of thought, freedom of expression, freedom of movement, freedom of work and trade. Freedom, as well as our relative – and maybe temporary – material success, attracts naturally people from all over the world – and they must be free and welcome to follow this attraction. In mutual respect, free to follow the customs of their culture strictly within the frame of the law of the land.

Now this civilisation is under attack. As it has already

been by Communism and Nazism. Because it is founded on freedom and diversity, it is attacked by totalitarian and supremacist ideologies. The most obvious of these threats is Political Islamism, tending to impose, on the pretext of religious supremacy, a moral and physical order that we think unbearable and that, indeed, many Muslims find excessive.

Another threat is the resurrection of the European fascist and neo-Nazi movements, as usual under the guise of "nationalism". We are, indeed, treading a very thin line between two evils. But we must keep going. Our heritage is freedom, diversity, tolerance, humanity. And we must defend it using the weapons that are in keeping with our ideals. This, I believe, must be clear to all.

Political institutions set the frame to our individual and diverse freedoms. This means fairness to all. Fair sharing of the collective wealth. Fair protection of the weakest. Fair dispensing of an education allowing all children to grow up into this civilisation, and exercise their own freedom. Fair justice – no crime, no offence, to be let unpunished, and punishment being In proportion to the charges. This is the least one can expect in England, the country of *habeas corpus*. Not the belonging to any community, not the following of any faith, not the tradition of any culture, may be an excuse for any crime. The law must be the same to all – and it must be seen as strict to be respected by all.

It is unbearable that children be used as sexual objects, it is unbearable that girls be forced into an early and unwilling marriage, it is unbearable that

young people of any community be denied the
freedom of other young people in the country, it is
unbearable that women be victims of domestic
violence or "honour crimes". There is no honour in
crime, not in our civilisation. It is unbearable that a
young man be savagely assassinated because he was a
soldier.

It is unbearable that people open fire from a car over
a political demonstration, as any political violence is
unacceptable.

It is unacceptable that a crowd should jeer troops
returning from combat. It is unacceptable that the
symbols and institutions of a country should be
insulted. It is unacceptable that anyone should use
their freedom of speech to call for the destruction of
the very country that hosts them, for the physical
elimination of its very political elite.

On the other hand, it is unacceptable that anyone
should propagate lies and hateful rumours against any
community within the country. We have known that
before... Jews, Christians, Masons, now Muslims,
have always been slandered. With all the strength of
modern information media, this slandering has
become extremely dangerous and must be met with
severity.

It is an easy temptation to charge a whole community,
even a nation, with the sins of some of its members.
We had thought that our civilisation had grown out of
this: nobody ever thinks of holding the German
people responsible for the crimes of Nazism. Yet

there are people who will insist that the whole Muslim community be responsible for the actions of criminal groups or of activist cells.

This is unacceptable. My Muslim friends have regular habits, regular families, they give their children as much care and education as they can. I am as much offended as they are when their entire community is accused of hateful child abuse. Street movements have an important part to play. They call up the attention of Government upon sensitive issues. They are definitely part of the freedom of a population to express ideas, fears, even anger. As part of the dignity of the people, they must keep their own dignity in the street and not fall into the gutter of hate.

They should reflect on this: insulting a whole community can only result in pushing the more sensitive members of that community under the influence of the activists and the criminals. So they produce an effect exactly to the contrary of what they want to achieve. This may be unpalatable to many. I hold it is a good point.

June, 2014

HATE IS NO SOLUTION

WE ARE ALL IN IT TOGETHER...

1

HERE A FREE MAN - THERE A MAN IN PRISON

Tuesday, 4th February 2014

I am a free man. It has taken me a long time to free myself of inbred prejudice and excessive reverence for status. I am here, free and I am 72. There, a young man is in prison. I have never seen him. We have little in common. Our chance encounter on a football evening in a pub would probably have resulted in our being thrown out by the landlord to sort out our differences.

He is in prison for something he has done against the law. I think, as an observer, that he has had a raw deal. I believe that a different man, with a different social background, taking a different stance in politics, might have been treated differently by the same court regarding the same offence.

The young man I have mentioned is Steven Yaxley Lennon - known to many as Tommy Robinson, and Tommy Robinson I shall call him hereafter.

Tommy Robinson has said "I grew up in Luton". He is a working class lad, challenging professional politicians to do their job instead of courting ballots. I believe that men from the working classes should carry more weight in politics. They should, in my country anyway. He has made two moves that have gained him my support:

Tommy Robinson was angered when he saw people in England demonstrating against English military units regressing from combat. These actions he saw as offences and lack of due respect to those who fight for their country, to the risk of their life. Such a reaction is honourable in all men, in all countries. He embarked on a course and founded a patriotic political organisation, the English Defence League. Then he discovered that patriotism could be infiltrated by nationalism, that his manly wrath could be spoiled by hate. He understood that an entire community should not be made to answer for acts of its more extreme members, but on the contrary, be protected against the illegitimate pressure of those extremists.

Then he made another move, smaller, but I believe that it was for him a giant step, and should have started a formidable current of communication, leading to understanding, and to respect between communities divided by dramatic issues. He withdrew from the English Defence League and opened a dialogue with a Muslim reflection group.

I am a soldier, I have been an instructor of men, and I believe that Tommy Robinson has shown the charisma and positive thinking of a chief of men. He has bravely crossed a bridge.

Between the hard-working, suffering, exasperated and bewildered working class of his country and the bewildered community of migrants, most of them come over only to have a better life, he stands alone, misunderstood and...Yes, hated. Against the political class, better educated, better dressed, better spoken, but lacking the capacity or will-power to solve a dramatic situation, he stands alone.

I want to help him with my feeble powers and experience. This is the purpose of writing this book.

2

<u>WHAT IS ENGLAND TO ME</u>

5th February

The year was 1956. The school was a good school. Not a posh one - a good school. Loughborough College School. The boys - well there WERE a few girls, but meaningless in numbers - were mostly middle class, upper working class, serious chaps. There were some expats' kids and very few foreigners. I was easily the most exotic one, and Matron, at roll-call, after glibly sounding easy names like *Suchin Baholyodhin* and *Milan Kumar Katiar*, never managed to call me anything but "French boy". To my pals I was "Pedro"…

I was a scrawny 15, the form was Middle Vth Sc. I

loved it. There was no school in France where one could take ironwork, woodwork and Latin in the same stride, play so much games, and be so well educated in community living, in respect of everyone's personality and character. History was taught us by an RAF officer who was also in command of ATC - in which I was permitted to enlist. This was England to me.

I came from the French lower middle class - my father a draughtsman, my mother a typist. We lived in Morocco, uncertain if we were migrants or expats. As things turned up, the family went back to the old country, not richer, but with a wealth of emotions and impressions that watermarked my personality.

I had been sent to Loughborough to learn English, because a man who worked with my Dad had a sister who lived there, married to an Englishman. Mr Thompson was a tall, solid, silent man, who drove a Norton bike with a side-car and smoked St Bruno's in his pipe. His mother, for me the quintessential English old lady, chain-smoked 3 boxes of Capstan cigarettes every day...

Those were the times of coke fires, dandelion beer, Jello pudding. It was post-war England. The Queen was a very young woman who rode side-saddle a gleaming chestnut horse on her official portraits. Her grandmother, Queen Mary, the most formidable woman of her time, had only been dead a few years, and was vividly remembered. One smoked at the pics and stood at attention for the National Anthem at the end of the show. Films from Ealing's Studios were the blockbusters of the times.

One had to apply Sioux-like stealth to go to the pics on a Sunday, not to be caught by Matron - a forceful lady who had been a driver in the war and married the Colonel – he was now our Headmaster; I still get a shiver down my spine when I remember dodging her patrolling car - grey and blue Hillman Minx, NJU 246. We were never severely punished, though, except by being gated for a week-end or two. My pals - I am still friends with some of them - were very patient with obnoxious me. I realise that, in all fairness, I should have had my bottom kicked and my nose hit more than once.

This was the country I grew to love. I did learn some English indeed during that year in Loughborough. Most of all, I got to admire the people of England, the honest, hardworking, patriotic people who had been through a severe ordeal as they bore alone the brunt of the terrible war against the Nazi horror.

Now I have committed myself to support Tommy Robinson, as a way to repay that youthful experience. It is possible that I be wrong. If so, I'll gladly pay the price. Any price. Because at my age I have nothing to lose, and that is how important England is for me, a country I grew to love and respect.

NO WORDS FOR IT

I have just heard that Tommy Robinson has been attacked in his prison. Thank goodness, they say it is just bruises, black eyes, bloodied nose. That

does not come as a surprise. It was common knowledge that he was liable to be attacked. It was anyone's guess that various people wished him to come to harm. Yet it happened. I have no doubt that the Ministry of Justice is taking this matter seriously.[1] However, it raises questions about prisoners' status. Just a few hours ago, I expressed my love for England, the country of my boyhood. I still love the people of England. I still respect this magnificent country. I still would fight for the Union Jack as for my own flag if necessary, under the common banner of Europe. But what is happening now I find hard to accept. I do not like the politicians who have let the situation deteriorate, I do not like the people who do not take legal and regular care of prisoners. I would not like to believe that Justice might be susceptible to political influence. Tommy Robinson is an Englishman. He is part of the England I love and honour. Even when, as a prisoner, he is paying a debt to society, he must be respected. And protected.

---

[1] Indeed, I received from the National Offender Management Service, HMP WOODHILL, a courteous letter by which the Head of Security and Intelligence, unable to confirm any details, could nevertheless assure me that "all matters of this nature (were) taken seriously and that the incident (...) (had) been subject to further enquiry".

3

ANGER GOOD - HATE BAD - KILLER WORDS

6th February, 2014

Years ago, I taught for three years running the officer-cadets of one of the French military academies a subject I called "informative writing". A blend of analyzing information and giving a clear account of it to whomever needed it. Usually a commander who had no time to listen but would never forgive not having being told. And in my first presentation, I insisted upon the facts that **WORDS KILL**.

Words that condemn a man to death or exile, words that arouse deadly feuds and mortal passions, words that start wars and violence and are unable to re-establish peace. Words of anger. Words of hate.

I am past the age of bodily fighting with any hope of bringing down a physical adversary. Which does not mean that I would not stand up eventually, to the trivial danger of spilling some blood. A small tribute to a cause. But this blog of words is my primary weapon.

I will not be one of those old armchair warriors, exciting the young to fight and encouraging them to die. I will not, either, call them to cowardice and acceptance of the unacceptable. I mean to use clear words, unambiguous facts, and my own experience, to clear up the path for peace among men, even at the cost of angry battles - because there are times when actual fighting becomes in order - "une juste guerre" in the words of the French patriotic poet Charles Péguy. - The problem is that no war can ever be totally justified. This is where words come in as expression of clear ideas or - on the contrary - as signs of perverse confusion of values.

The most dangerous confusion is between ANGER and HATE.

ANGER is when blood rushes to the face of a man as he sees his family, his land, his country, his flag, his friends, his companions-at-arms threatened, defiled, attacked. It is a reaction against hostile actions. It flares up as an urge to punish the attacker and vindicate the victim. I am no philosopher. I am an old soldier refusing to fade away. I think anger is a terrible but honourable passion in a man.

HATE is completely different. It is not directed at any precise threat or any individual foe, but extends to a whole category of people, because of their link - real or supposed - with a threat - real or supposed - . It rests on what it called, I believe, a sophism: "Socrates was a man. Socrates is dead. Therefore all men are dead".

ANGER stands up. HATE crawls and creeps, sowing seeds of subsequent hates around it.

ANGER is a noble passion, HATE is a disease of the soul.

ANGER rises from the heart, HATE flows from the gallbladder.

Tommy Robinson started his enthusiastic career on ANGER. He understood that some were turning it into HATE and went on fighting. He aroused more HATE against him. That HATE has brought about the ugly attack of yesterday.

This attack has in turn aroused the ANGER of many of us - irrespective of their adhering or not to Tommy's ideas - We must act and I am certain we shall act to ensure that the cowards who executed the attack, and the criminals who ordered it or let it happen, be punished.

But our ANGER must be directed against the guilty only. It would be ugly and sad if it became HATE.

Because HATE does not stop with victory, HATE goes on and on, poisoning every mind and body.

I think it would be honourable - and respectful of Tommy Robinson's angry and legitimate commitment, not to let this loathsome event create more hate yet between communities. Because I know that many innocent people would die, whose only wish is to live in peace.

I do realise that this post will arouse some anger among my friends. That's all right! I'll face that... whatever form it takes! Just remember: we are here because we want TOMMY ROBINSON safe and free.

4

PATRIOT AND
NATIONALIST

8th February

Tommy Robinson has now been transferred to a safer prison and this is good news. When he has served his time, he will be back and carry on. His followers and his friends will loyally continue their support. I shall continue this blog as long as I may, and it will become a book - hopefully short - that may be a tool and a weapon for him - if he will.

I am certain of only two things: Steven Yaxley-Lennon, as a working-class man who has had more of the rough than of the smooth, has the qualities to lead and serve his fellow-countrymen. Tommy Robinson, who has had the courage of founding EDL and the perhaps greater courage of leaving it, has the sort of pragmatic honesty that many politicians lack - everywhere. I believe his tentative gesture towards a Muslim organisation is a clear sign that he wants to solve problems, not impose solutions.

I mean to continue pouring into this blog the little knowledge I have accumulated in my years and travels, of men, of ideas and of words. For him to use. Or not.

Words about words may seem childish or donnish. It is not. If one is prepared to fight for his ideals, and to support his beliefs with his life, one had better know what one is talking about.

Indifferent use of words induces a comedy of errors, that may soon be a tragedy of mistakes.

Thus: patriotism and nationalism are often used as substitutes - and they should not. Someone has said: **"Patriotism is about loving one's country, Nationalism is about hating other countries"**. This, I think, is true.

I have been a soldier, training young men from all stations in life and all origins to defend our country. It was my choice, it was my duty. Mine not to reason why, mine but to do and serve. I would let no one question my patriotism.

Out of uniform, however, those who know me are aware that I have always antagonised nationalism. Since I came of age and got my right to vote - more than half a century ago - I have felt committed to a more open vision of my country. Open to immigrants who were the grandsons of men who fought in never-to-be-forgotten wars. Open to our neighbours, to forget and mutually forgive centuries of absurd wars in Europe. Open to other cultures, because I am proud enough of my culture to believe it can resist contact with even the most uncongenial - and even benefit from it.

Nationalism is part of the darkest heritage of the French Revolution and of the subsequent attempt by Napoleon I to mould the whole of Europe into the rigid frame of centralisation. Nationalism, however, is a double-edged sword: It means freedom for those who feel oppressed by a power so distant as to be felt foreign. It means also hostility to any contact from the outside that is perceived as a threat. From this ambiguity of nationalism arises the real danger. It is often first perceived as a poor man's revenge on life, and only when it is too late it is discovered to be in fact the war machine of a would-be aggressor. A perfect example is Nazism (national-socialism) that arose from the genuine disgrace of down-trodden Germany in 1919, and became the cruel madness that sent millions of innocent civilian people into the gas-chambers. Why did the German people support it? Because it played on the patriotism of the soldiers of WW1, using old Hindenburg as a cover as long as they could. Why did the other Powers accept it? We know there are many reasons, but one of them is that the International Community felt responsible for the terrible state Germany was in the 1920's.

Patriotism is about standing up for one's colours.

Nationalism is about using one's colours as a decoy to prey on the most vulnerable. Great Britain, as I know it, love it and respect it, is one of the most patriotic countries in the world. It has never known nationalism - except in the 1930's with a small fraction of people - hardly from the working class - that were admirers of Hitler.

Tommy Robinson walked out of EDL and towards some sort of discussion with a community that he has reasons to perceive as hostile. It was certainly a difficult decision for him. I believe it was the right decision, and that small step was in fact a giant step away from nationalist temptations, back to patriotism.

I respect him for it. Hugely.

5

THE HILL

9th February

She's the mother of two rivers
That hill.
To the East runs one gentle stream
In peace.

As quietly flows another brook
Westwards.
Two men were born on the same day
Near by.

One to the East, one to the West
Both men.
They went to town, looking for work
And met.

They were brothers in homesickness
Those men
Recalling what they missed most
The hill.

How glorious in the setting sun
Said one
You blind fool, it's the morning
dawn
You mean.

They flashed knives and so they bled
To death
The hill is best in truthful light
At noon.

6

RACISM

In 1979, I went to the USA - to spend six months in a military school, as a guest of that awesome country. Once there, I had to fill a form - don't remember what for - where I was asked MY RACE. I was outraged. Such a question in France was (and is), improper and against the Constitution. I found it offensive. I demurred. I was told it was that or nothing. Then... I WAS A COWARD. I wanted very much to spend those six months in the South-West. I knew the Army at home would not take it kindly if I chucked it away and took first plane back. So I put myself down "*caucasian*".

Shame on me.

Racism is a crime against the Declaration of Rights, racism is a crime against human reason, racism lies deep down in the subconscious of all the nationalisms, all the fascisms, all the totalitarianisms.

Racism is the greatest evil of those times. Worse even than religious fanaticism, precisely because they team up easily. The wars of "Christians" vs "Muslims" in Central Africa are often tribal feuds re-kindled by religious proselytism. And it is always here, right in our midst, hidden under polite words like "nationalism" or "identitarianism". Bullshit.

Animals have a natural fear of the unknown and different. Humans are animals capable of rational thought. Racists are those who, instead of educating their fellow-humans to suppress that basic fear, cultivate it and turn it into a systematic rejection of whomever doesn't fit into their so-called racial standard.

In that year 1979, in New Orleans, I boarded an empty bus and sat in the middle - as I pleased. When the bus filled up I saw with surprise that all the passengers - all coloured - rushed to sit well behind me, leaving all the seats empty in the front. I realised with horror that, almost twenty-five years after the Rosa Parks case, I could feel the scars of racism in that bus. Maybe they expected me to get up and sit in front, but that I could not.

Dear fucking racists, do me a favour: whatever the

race you think you belong to - always to consider me as one of the opposite party. The party of those who own to no discrimination among humans whatever their line of ancestry, place of birth, colour of skin, gender, orientation, philosophy or birthplace.

NOW WHO'S RACIST?

"Racist" is probably the widely used disparaging word to-day. It is used to stop any proceedings against a person, as soon as there the least suspicion of discrimination. I mean negative discrimination. Because positive discrimination is accepted as a pious and bigoted version of equitable treatment. Now I do not agree. A man is a man. No less. No more. The law is the same for all. Or must be.

I don't call racist the person who just does not feel comfortable in the presence of someone else whose difference is perceived as a shock. When a person looks at me askance because I am walking my dogs and that person is afraid of dogs, I don't call her "dog-owner-hater". I just tighten visibly my grip on the leash and move a little apart, not to offend. That is not racism or antiracism, it is common courtesy.

I call racist the persons or bodies that build up false theories of supremacy founded on differences in blood ancestry, geographical origin, skin colouring, cultural practices, language, clothing... these theories have been invented in the 19th century as a justification for colonial exploitation of those masses who did not have industrial capacities, by the nations who had these capacities - Well... Europe and North America.

These theories have been largely used, applied, enforced as laws, by the Nazi state in Germany and - until the mid-1950's in the United States of America. Watered down, they have served as support to unjust colonisation of Africa by the French, the Portuguese, the Belgians, even the British (the least racist of people). Remains of these theories still linger everywhere - European cabinet ministers, who happen to have African forebears, have been - and daily are - grossly insulted on account of their physical appearance and blood ancestry. This has to stop. This I mean to fight.

But racism goes deep into the malignity of the human social soul: As the pendulum of History has swung back, a reverse racism has appeared. It is not less a racism because it applies in another direction. I will never call a man "nigger" or "bougnoule". I am not letting anyone call me "whitey" or "babtou" - except as a friendly joke from a mate.

Racism is not about not liking other people, Racism is about giving oneself the right not to like other people because of their "race" - whatever that be. This is evil. This is stupid. This goes against both reason and justice. There is only one race of humans: the human race.

In France, people with exotic names have trouble getting interviewed for a job. It has been proposed that resumes be made anonymous - with no reference AT ALL to any criteria that could lead to discrimination. It certainly is one solution. But the real solution is to EDUCATE people at all levels against racism, and teach them - not force them - to accept differences. Because this is a small planet, becoming smaller, and we have to live together or die.

7

NOT GUILTY, MY LORD!

12th February

No, this is not a joke about a mate of us who is now residing in one of HM's prisons. It would be indelicate. I take the opportunity to wish him strength and courage - though I know he has plenty of that. Keep going, Tommy Robinson, don't let anyone steer you from your course. Not even me!!!

I only mean to reflect on the extraordinary taste for self-flagellation in a civilisation that sprang from Judeo-Christianity and has bloomed into Socialism and Communism. The build-up of the Western guilt complex is a most extraordinary - and I believe unprecedented - paradigm of collective suicide. That civilisation (ours, as surprising as it may be) is guilty of countless actions that are considered crimes according to our state-of-the-art morals. Therefore, our loins covered in sackcloth, must be totter on our knees, under the whiplashes of the Angel of History, towards the final day of Expiation.

This is **bullshit**. As it is endorsed by respectable persons, I'll call it respectable **bullshit**. It is even Biblical **bullshit:** something about parents having eaten sour grapes and children's teeth being on edge. It is still **bullshit.** It is convenient **bullshit** for political leverage. It is still ... **BULLSHIT.**

If man's most treasured possession be freedom of choice, he is fully responsible for his actions or inactions but may not be made to account for the passive or active offences of others. Not on any base. The modern Athenian is no more responsible for the sack of Troy than the modern French for the sack of the Palatinate or the sack of Rome, nor the present-day Roman for the sack of Jerusalem in the year 70.

Slavery is a crime against humanity. It still exists in some countries. It may be argued that in many more countries even the conditions of work are a form of slavery. It must be fought NOW, not in the past. So of Colonization. So of Genocide. Dear young West-Indian friend, dear young Native American friend, dear young Algerian friend, dear young Jewish friend, do not look at me with that irate expression. I wasn't born when your African ancestor was sold by a slave-trader, I wasn't born when the hypocritical and cynical Puritans tried to exterminate the tribes who welcomed them, I wasn't born when your land was taken by force and given to the Alsatian refugees of the Franco-German war in 1871. I had no part in the various pogroms of Europe and none in the Nazi extermination camps. The memory of those crimes galls in everyone's memory. Those who committed them were responsible - Those who looked on and let them happen are responsible. A few survivors still have to pay. But it is an injustice to have the living pay for the dead, the innocent for the guilty.

This is so clear that the Ancient Jews had invented the Scapegoat to clean up memories of past deeds that cannot be undone. The Christians refined upon that with the dogma of Redemption. Both translate the same idea that guilt is not a heirloom to be handed down to generation after generation. The past cannot be mended. It must be built upon, and lessons must be taken from its patterns. We can't help what has happened. But we can and must prevent it to happen again. I will not answer for past injustice. But, being aware of it would make my guilt heavier if I committed or condoned new injustice. Of that I should answer to my conscience, to a court, to the opinion of my fellow-men, to God.

I plead **not guilty** of the past of my country, I plead **not guilty** of the past of my civilisation. I plead **not guilty** of the past of the religion in which I was raised. But, my Lord, I would plead **guilty** to the present and ask for no mitigation, if I did not protest against, and fight injustice with whatever means I have, when the people of country are denied their rights by a state that does not abide with international law.

I rest my case...

8

THE COLONEL'S LADY AND
JUDY O'GRADY

I am past 70. I have done things. Some perhaps good, more than adequately rewarded. Some certainly bad, for which I escaped punishment - yet. I have been places. I have met people. What strikes me most, when I think back, is that differences don't mean much. Under different skin colouring, different clothing, immersed in different cultures, following different politics, people are much more alike than they would care to admit.

In 1975 I was posted to Portugal to liaise with the Army of that country. I was a youngish captain, just down from commanding a training unit of the French forces in Germany. I was invited to visit one unit, back from the war in Africa, and that had taken no mean part in the Revolutionary process. There was a platoon on training - I remember, they were doing mine detection. I watched them. Suddenly, I felt I could have put a name on each and every soldier on the platoon, including the highly trained Sergeant, so much did their attitude remind me of attitudes of men I had known before. This has made me a life-friend of Portugal. More, it has taught me that it was more important, and probably more respectful, to look for resemblance instead of looking for difference.

The tourist's eye, in need of exoticism, is unbearably idiotic. It is often unconsciously insulting. As dear Miss Marple would say: (perhaps the younger don't know her, she's that wonderful character of a village old lady invented by Agatha Christie who solves countless mysteries) "my dear... **people are so very much the same everywhere...**" They are. In every group of people one can find the same types - the fighter, the coward, the well-meaning, the mean, the mad preacher, the wise person. In every community of human beings, there is a very large number of people who mean well and just want to live in peace and breed their children, and work, and better their lives. And there is a small number of evil ones who are greedy for power and influence, and ready to use any kind of means to get those.

I am now translating into English a book by an Algerian writer - that should be out in the UK before Summer; it tells the story of how a young man got himself caught in the circuits of violent terror, and how he succeeded in turning the tide of terror, helped to eliminate the evil ones, and re-establish peace in his community. It is an extremely violent story, and I believe it is extremely well informed... I know already of one young man in England, whom I shall present this book to. In fact I was thinking of him when I embarked on this translation. Of course this man is Tommy Robinson, who has begun to realize that the most important thing is to cut out the evil self-appointed leaders from the community they terrorise, and whom I believe is capable of **turning the tide.**

TIME AND PLACE
MAKE ALL THE DIFFERENCE

Some good, some bad, most indifferent... This is my vision of human nature, pretty much the same everywhere. Humans are driven by the will to survive and the scare of dying, and tend to move in herds or packs, as sheep and wolves do. People are pretty much the same everywhere. This is what makes war, and hate, so stupid.

The way they organize to survive and master their fears, however, may be very different from place to place. Because the Earth is not a nice, smooth piece of land offering equal opportunities to both hunter and tiller, miner and sailor, sheep or wolf. Any community is marked by the circumstances of its appearance. A tribe of nomadic shepherds moving between Nile and Euphrates may NOT respond to environmental threats as a village of fishermen in Alaska. Of course geography and climate and resources WILL make a difference.

Homo is not only supposed to be wise or *sapiens*, it is also essentially *faber;* a naked ape, vulnerable by its very erectness, Man has had to invent tools for everyday life. This is what makes history. Communities will develop specific tools – the wheel, say, or the steam engine, or computer science – but they will not develop the same tools at the same time everywhere. Of course this is obvious, and it is NOT a matter of superior efficiency or intelligence: it is a matter of appropriate response in different situations to the basic will to survive (and, may we say, of toiling less to enjoy more)

At the same time, human communities have had to address the fear of Death. This is another difference from our fellow animals: that spark of metaphysics that leads to the vital interrogation of eternity. The output of that, of course, is religion. Priests, wise men in all communities, under inspiration or not, have given an answer that they thought appropriate – and generally soothing – to that terrible question of giving a meaning to death.   Such answers have been adopted, and adapted, to each particular community, so as to be part of their identity.

Religion and technique, as they made life easier, made relationships inside the community more complicated. They competed and combined to organise what is called civilised life: Public morality and law and order – and the ownership of the means of production. Thus, in each community, the State, the Priest, the Entrepreneur, the Worker, formed a special blend of all the qualities and failings of the human race, which, in the course of time, was shaped by the normal power struggles that we inherited from our animal ancestors.

No two communities could ever have developed the same answers to their different situations.

As addressing a problem – be it solving it or making it worse – changes its terms, it stands to reason that the rules of problem-solving have had to change in the course of time. By this I mean that the ownership of the means of production may have changed, that religion, public morality and law may have changed in the course of time.

After WW1, pessimistic thinkers, as Spengler, or Paul Valéry, warned us that "civilisations could die" – even, that any civilisation was doomed. This galls, of course. It is, however, an indication that their span of life necessarily includes changes, from growth to decline. It is, I believe, a good idea to take into account the AGE of a civilization if one wants to compare it with another.

Islam, for instance, lives in the year of Hegira 1435. Rough times. Quarrels between rival schools of thought. We are shocked. Just remember what was the state of affairs in Christendom in the 15th century? Just remember, in England, how Protestants and Catholics failed to live harmoniously together under Queens Elizabeth and Mary.

Although human nature is pretty much the same everywhere, we must remember that time and place have made all the differences, and that the fast globalization of our time is breaking all the protective barriers of all the civilisations in the world.

This is why HATE IS NO SOLUTION. I do not suggest permissiveness, laxity, weakness – on the contrary. Any community in its internationally recognized space must be firm on its principles and its independence. But wherever and whenever they meet, I advocate Tolerance. Understanding. Getting to know the person opposite. Getting to TALK and explain. What Tommy Robinson has been trying to do – and, I trust, will go on doing as soon as he may.

.

9

What is an *"INTERNATIONALE OF NATIONALISTS"?*

16th February

I am very puzzled at the international gathering of parties who call themselves nationalists. It does not make sense that a French party that makes great show of devotion to the tri-colour flag should entertain brotherly relationship with movements in Austria or Germany perceived as close to the ideology and memory of Nazism. Also, if I understand that young men of energetic disposition be attracted to the flamboyant romanticism of the Spanish Falange, I remember being a boy in Franco's Spain and getting insulted daily because I was French. Last, when I see an English patriot being patted on the back by the most vocal groups of the French far right, I feel that, perhaps, misunderstandings are at the base of these temporary understandings, which bodes ill for the future.

Most of the French far right ideas spring not from the healthy anger of patriotism, but from bigoted conservatism and the yellowest forms of xenophobia and hate.

The French far right dig their roots deep into absolutism and fundamentalist Catholicism. The seeds of hate and distrust sowed during the terribly mismanaged Revolution have never ceased to grow in a nation ever attracted by the trappings of civil war – though carefully avoiding the real thing. Many heavy and clever books having certainly been written on the subject, I shall only sketch out in this blog my personal reasons for not liking very much the "Extrême Droite". They are quite welcome to reciprocate.

I was one of them. At 18 I sported the "fleur de lys" on my lapel, attended dusky meetings in dusty bookshops, ground my teeth when the Jews or the Masons, were mentioned –usually together- and said prayers to St Joan of Arc. Then I grew up. I found they were wrong, and my now large span of life has strengthened my conviction, and my hostility. That perhaps makes a traitor of me in their eyes. I don't care: other and better men have been called traitors, only because they stood fast to their idea of justice and patriotism.

10

ANTI-SEMITISM:

THE BLACK CLOUD.OVER THE FRENCH RIGHT

17th February

In 1870, the incapacity of military command drove France into disaster in the short war against Prussia. Prussia became the German Empire, France lost two provinces, Alsace and Lorraine, and had to pay enormous war damages. Moreover, the insurrection of the Commune de Paris, fiercely repressed by the transition government, created a general climate of hate between the urban working class and the bourgeois state. As usual, the nation looked for suitable scapegoats.

In those years of triumphant capitalism, engineers, entrepreneurs, banks and sharks made and lost fortunes. The middle class, as greedy but less lucky, were lured into mythic investments that turned out to be gigantic frauds. Hate crystallised against the bankers and – clearly – the Jews. Anti-Semitism was rampant everywhere, and certainly not limited to the conservatives, but as it was everywhere, it could materialise nowhere. Until the Dreyfus case in 1894.

A great novel by Robert Harris "An Officer and A Spy" gives a most acceptable outline of that case. Captain Alfred Dreyfus was arrested and convicted of spying for Germany. He was innocent, but could not free himself of the charge without endangering national security. Then, he was a Jew, and public opinion flared up against him and his people. This is one of the saddest phases of French History, when the entire world watched incredulously a great nation divided against itself, until the Cour de Cassation, after ten long years, had Dreyfus rehabilitated. He was given back his *Légion d'Honneur*, served in WW1 and died a Colonel – His widow had to hide from the Nazis in a French nunnery during WW2.

This has left deep scars even now. The French right had rallied around the military, against the "Jewish Traitor" and the resulting trend of anti-Semitism was so strong that even solid patriots, after the capitulation of 1940, turned collaborationists. Part of the French nationalists still retain that spirit of hate, switching easily from anti-Semitism to any kind of xenophobia. Nazi symbols, or symbols of the Vichy Régime, barely made acceptable by subtle changes, are stencilled or tattoo-d wherever those men gather and parade.

Merely ignoring them may not be forever enough to rid France of that nefarious breed.

FRENCH NAZI-LOVERS: STOCKHOLM SYNDROME

Part of the French far-right has a sickly obsession with Nazi Germany that originates in a sort of Stockholm syndrome: losers admiring winners.

During the last-stand wars in Indo-China and Algeria, all patriotic admiration in France went to the Foreign Legion, which indeed was admirable in skill, bravery and discipline. A great number of former troops of the defeated German army had found refuge there. They were the best and they knew it. The French could not but admire them and be inspired by them. Even in campfire songs and paratroopers' marches. "Of course, the German army is what we admire, not the Nazis", would the more educated French military hasten to say. I am not even sure they fooled themselves.

There is in Nazi German lore something that appeals to the French professional soldiers: the worship of male body and a taste for parades. Politicians could say that the defeat of 1940 was due to the imbecility senile commanders, or – to the contrary – that support and supply had been sabotaged by the treacherous Left, but soldiers saw only what they could see: the Germans used well their equipment and made a great show of both individual fitness and unit cohesion.

This respect became a sort of cult for the mythical blond Aryans parading in Nuremberg or dipping naked into the Bavarian lakes to show off their perfect muscles. As France accumulated defeats in her soon-to-be-lost Empire, despite the courage and quality of her troops, the lockers of young officers and sergeants accumulated fetishes that should never have been tolerated. But they were "good boys" with winning, open faces, and weakling commanders shrugged away their responsibility.

A few weeks ago, a good soldier in one of the best regiments was photographed in Africa, sporting a badge with a motto on it – in German. A beautiful motto, no doubt of it, very full of "honour" and "glory". Except that it was a Gestapo motto. This case has shown how deeply that admiration of Nazi-German lore has penetrated French youth, precisely where it should be more patriotic; this is one of the poisons that make the French Far Right extremely toxic.

THE ALGERIAN CURSE

The stand of France on immigration is flawed by the sad truth and tragic consequences of France's mismanagement of the Algerian drama – let us say 1936-1962.

The French emigrated towards Algeria. Then their offspring had to return to France. And later Algerians became immigrants in France. These were bulky shifts of population. The repatriation of settlers in 1962 dealt with close to 2% of the population of

France and 10% of that of Algeria. Algerian immigrants, in 2005, accounted for 0.7% or the entire population of France. Figures, however, are less important than people and their feelings or resentments.

Technically French citizens of second rate, native Algerians voted separately. The educated elite claimed equality, but in 1936, a few influent and affluent settlers blocked a law that gave equal voting right to the native population.

As France capitulated before Hitler in 1940, a free French Army, with the support of the British and the Americans, was set up with colonial troops and eventually played a most significant part in the final victory. 1945 should have given an opportunity for changing the rules and giving equal dignity to former colonies. As the British had the sense to do in the Indian subcontinent.

Instead, France tried to impose a continuation of the colonial rules, at the cost of military operations that left terrible scars. Finally, De Gaulle, as ungrateful to the North African troops as to his British and American allies, rid France of Algeria and passed the buck over to a totalitarian, incompetent, communist-style regime, that led itself to Islamic revolt and terror. Thence, a continuous flow of Algerian immigrants into France.

There is bad blood, naturally, between the offspring of the settlers that came back in 1962 in tragic conditions, and the new population of immigrants.

This makes a very rough sea indeed, on which the Far Right enjoys surfing. But the responsibility is not on the immigrants, nor on the returned settlers, but on the successive governments of fifty years who never paid any attention to a situation that could easily be foreseen.

Slogans and demos will not solve a problem that can only be taken with respect for all sides, mutual understanding, and accepting unpalatable truths.

11

MY FIRST MEAL IN A MUSLIM HOME

19th February

Yesterday I had words with a good friend from East Anglia. Obviously we do not see eye to eye about Islam. I shall suggest a reason for that, and tell a story about my first real experience with Muslims, half a century ago.

I was born French in Morocco – a Muslim kingdom. Those were colonial times and I had been trained to… well… ignore that majority of Muslims who lived around me in their country. I moved to France for college in 1958 but as my folks still lived and worked in Casablanca, it was still my home for holidays for many years.

In 1965, I was an officer cadet at Saint Cyr Military Academy. I had a pal from Morocco who asked me to visit his father there as he'd use his holidays to enjoy French... company. The father was an old gentleman, both well-educated in the French style and a learned one in Islam (an 'Alem). We met in town, then he took me home to share the evening breakfast of Ramadan (*ftouh* or *iftar*). As he introduced me to his wife, I could not conceal some surprise, as I believed in all the current clichés. The gentleman smiled and said: "as you come from our son, it is but proper that his mother greet you". The lady sat at table with us. Younger sons served us – and, well, that day I really learnt to respect Muslim traditions and culture.

I have said before that, although human nature be the same everywhere, time and place makes a difference. I do understand that history, geography and local situation makes quite a difference between equally respectful and respectable Muslims. As they make a difference between, say, a Canon of Barchester and a fanatic monk in a French hysterical convent. Religion matters less than men, and there are good men everywhere.

Bad ones too... Those must be taken care of, wherever and whenever. No tolerance for them. But the people around them must not suffer for it. This I believe.

I don't say I hold absolute truth. I say that nobody does. Of course that makes me a miscreant with the Church in which I was brought up, with the learned ones of the Jewish Faith, and of course with the learned ones of Islam, not to forget the learned atheists and, of course, that illiterate moronic maniac of a parson in Florida who already wants to burn me alive for being gay.

All right. Take a number.

12

RESPECT

20th February

Years ago, when I taught methodology and written expression to officer-cadets in our Military Academies, I started one year's course with a simple test. I asked everyone to pen 100 words about "Respect". It was a disaster. All very formally and correctly explained how important it was for a soldier to respect the number above. No one. Repeat, NOT ONE, out of some 200 young men and women, all carefully selected and highly motivated for the Army, expressed any idea that respect was not a one-way affair, that you could not ask for it without giving it first.

Anyone who has taken part in or watched a bout of fencing, a boxing match, knows how important it is to show respect to each other before engaging the fight.

It is a despicable officer who despises his men. It is a despicable fighter who despises his adversary.

The modern way of respecting the enemy is not to play down his power, nor exaggerate his cunning and viciousness. It is to understand what he really is up to, and what his real strengths and weaknesses are. Hitler's tanks were not cardboard, nor were all his soldiers 7ft tall. Warfare is about anticipation, not imagination.

This blog is about anger and hate, about communities living together, about ethnic and religious differences. Let us not beat about the bush, it is about Islam in Britain, about a tense situation that takes sometimes the aspect of war, that carries already some of the tragic effects and threats of war; a situation that no sane person would like to see develop into any stronger form of violence.

A friendly foreigner in England, a friend to many Muslims, I believe that a better perception of Islam would help – and also a more thoughtful vision of what it means to be an immigrant – or simply someone different.

Why don't I go preach my stuff in my country? Good point. There are many similar points indeed, but things are often better understood when seen from a distance. Also, I am not convinced that any of the professional politicians who talk about immigration have a real desire to improve the situation. Here in

England I have found men who try to solve the problem, not just make a theory about it and get voters. I want to help. I come here to put facts, experience and ideas on the table and defend the case. I don't care if my nose gets punched. I am confident.

13

MIGRANTS CAN NEVER GO BACK

21st February

There is a solid trend in the richer countries of Europe to throw the guilt of their difficulties on immigrants and their offspring. Trend-sniffing political parties find it easier to demonstrate against immigration than to propose real problem-solving measures. "Immigrants go home" is a slogan that "sells" – no doubt of it.

This will not work, simply because immigrants have no home to go back to. Home to them is but the place where they have chosen to live. Emigration has created a chasm that can never be closed. Remember one has to emigrate before immigrating. Sounds silly, but it is the truth.

To emigrate is to cut oneself from one's past, from one's forebears and from one's friends. The process of emigrating begins later: at the landing of a plane, or of a boat, or at the crossing of a border. Find a job, find a place to live, learn a new way of life, often a new language. If you think it is easy, try it.

There is no going back. Even expats – limited time immigrants – are not at ease when they come back. The country to which one reverts is never the same as the country from which one has gone. Returning expats are never popular with their original countrymen.

Why do people emigrate? Pundits will write lengthy and weighty books about it. But it all amounts to one thing: to have a better life for themselves and their kids. As simple as that. This is natural. This is brave, too. They want to get better material conditions, for sure. Who doesn't? They choose a country where they believe they may find more safety and comfort, a country into which settling down will be easier. Who wouldn't?

The accusation that they only come to "scrounge benefits" is mean and insulting. It is also false, because the migrant's psychology– even with the most timid of them – is adventurous. To acquire freedom, not to seek protection. They want to adhere to the lifestyle of the new country, and if there are benefits to claim, why not claim them? But benefits can NEVER be the primary motive for the difficult decision of emigrating.

So politicians should just forget immigration-bashing, and roll-up sleeves and tackle the real problems of injustice, poverty, education and peace. This is harder for sure. But this is what they are paid for.

14

GREATNESS UNIQUE

22nd February

Encompassing the world, and yet
Present within the tiniest cell

Who has no name or has them all
Tho' some of them may be greater

Who is mightier than the mightiest
And yet humbler than the humblest

The Wrathful one – and Merciful
Who may destroy and who shall spare

Who is all things to all creatures
Father to Son, Son to Father

Who has spoken and is not heard
But lets us free to take our course

To whom only free men must bow
Only the One is great – Amen.

15

HATE MAKES ME ANGRY

23rd February

I have read so many tweets of hate and insult yesterday… All over the week-end I have been pelted with so much information of violence, hate and killings… For so many years I have kept my head down in a wind of stupidity, prejudice, ignorance and ill-will… That I want to shed the trappings of good education that were given to me – often against my will – such a long time ago – was it?

My anger is stronger against those who are nearer me. Against those who share the most of my culture, language, even blood ties. I am a European man, I express myself in European languages, I was brought up in the predominant faith of the country of my parents – Roman Catholicism, I was taught in the laws of the so-called Western civilisation.

So it is those closest and dearest to me that anger me most by making fools of themselves.

I shall never see another person as an enemy just because that person be different. I believe it is criminal to assess a person according to whatever group or community they belong. I believe every individual must answer for his own actions, not hide behind his folk, and no one has a right to challenge the folk on account of individual crime.

Those who commit a crime must be punished – whatever the community they belong to – in accordance to the laws of the country where the crime has been committed.

Family or tribal solidarity on crime are not accepted in our European world. Why should some of us decide that they should be applied now, to people who have come from outside – precisely to live in our world?

It is contrary to all Western ethics to generalise to many the guilt of a few. It is not acceptable, when charging or convicting someone for a crime, to stress that person's membership of any community.

A murder has been committed. Shut the murderer away for as long as law permits. I am not an advocate of relaxed laws and softened penalties.

Far from it. Even to myself…

But don't burn a village because of a man – we have grown out of that. And stop pointing at Islam whenever a Muslim commits an offence. Because Islam should be respected as any religion and any Muslim is as respectable as the beer-soaked lout who cries out vengeance, hate and prejudice.

A MAN IS A MAN. NO MORE. NO LESS.

16

YES I BELIEVE IN GOD – SO WHAT?

24th February

The process is simple:

1) Pin up a crime against some member of any community, then point out that the whole community is criminal.
2) Find what other communities share with the first one. Then attack all communities sharing this particular point.

Some Muslims have committed crimes, then All Muslims are criminals. Muslims believe in God, then all those who believe in God are criminals.

FUCK THE POLITICALLY CORRECT AGGRESSIVE ATHEISM OF GOD-HATING MILITANTS.

I was baptised and confirmed a Catholic. For reasons my own I have decided not to follow anymore the Church's teaching, nor to pay any lip-service to it.

I respect the religious forms that my parents and grandparents respected. They were good people, working people. Somewhere, aesthetically and sentimentally, those forms still move me.

I believe animals have no metaphysical interrogations. I have. I find an answer in "some spirit" that may have originated creation, and subsequent evolution. I do not hold it as truth, but I challenge any of those self-appointed great minds, to give me proof that this is not true. We are working on hypotheses, mine is as good as theirs. I do not accept proselytism; any way.

Just you fuckers let me alone.

As far as I know – and I am not THAT ignorant – all three monotheistic religions share the same basic answer to the Great Question – though of course their theologians have refined upon it. I don't need those refinements of theology and exegesis. At my own risk. I don't hold with proselytism and conversions. Religion is part of one's culture, you can't change that as you buy a new coat. I believe in respect. Mutual respect. Muslims and Christians talking and respecting each other.

That's all, for to-day.

17

WHAT IS IN A RELIGION?

25th February

Religion is the organisation of a number of people sharing a similar perception of a higher essence, from which emanates the world, and accepting common rules to relate to that higher essence.

In the beginning was Fear.
This fragile, naked ape, who developed a monstrous brain instead of healthy limbs, claws and teeth, as it became more and more a reasoning creature, tried to find an explanation for the felt hostility of nature – and for its own singularity.   He resolved his basic metaphysics problem with pantheism. Propitiating the trees, the hills, the stones, the rivers, the clouds in the sky, was a vital necessity. Animals, too, were godlike creatures to be appeased – until man found a way to kill them or tame them.

Later, as man understood that it was not so frail after all, it created gods to its own likeness - bearded gods or fleshy goddesses –. That was polytheism, magnificently illustrated by the jolly wars of the Greek gods or the crepuscular epics of German legend. Then some eastern tribes, wandering in the desert, felt an awesome sentiment of cosmic unity – and understood the futility of manlike divinities. Thus was monotheism born, from something that can truthfully be called a Revelation.

Successive revelations – and the squabbling nature of the now clothed ape – have divided monotheism into three branches: the original Judaism or Mosaism, Christianism, and Islam. The three of them account for about one half of the world's population. Islam is certainly the largest. It is also the newest, and that with the youngest population. It is no wonder that it should show the stronger tendency to expand.

All expansion meets with resistance. One particularly inadequate form of resistance has appeared in countries, like France and the U.K., small in population but very proud of past achievements, in the form of well-meaning advice. Pundits – that is the superior variety of mankind: the **gowned ape** – in doctoral tones tell Religions to "change their outlook on life", "reform the Church", "expel activist preachers".

Conceited and stupid… Any intrusion into these large structured bodies that religions are is necessarily – and justly – resented by its members, even by the great majority of those who would rather agree with the reforms suggested. This is what happens in the most obvious manner with the RC church in France, as well as with Islam in the UK and in France. An Englishman's house is his castle – well: so is a Muslim's mosque. Don't meddle.

A nation lives either in a secularised state or under the rules of a dominant religion. This is a choice to be respected. Take it or leave it. Personally I am in favour of a secularised state – always lived in one. When I visit a country where religion weighs on politics – and I do that rather often – I adapt. When rules are clear, it is not very difficult to comply. Rules, however, must be clear and unbiased.

If the rule is freedom of mind and speech, what is said inside a mosque, a church, a temple, a synagogue is no business of the secular State. Now crime is, definitely, the state's business. Crime is qualified and penalised by law. Most of the energy squandered in discussing religions from the outside should be concentrated in a fair, equal, and rigorous application of the Law. Never minding what is inside religion.

The law must reflect justice – protection of the weakest – not prejudice – custom and trend. Murder is murder. Child molesting is child molesting. Heinous crimes. Theft, embezzlement, fraud, are crimes. Not quite in the same line I believe. It is a country's privilege to decide between the relative importance of offences, to set up a balance between blood, money, freedom and dignity.

18

NO BURQA LAW!

26th February

Yesterday, I believe, Mr Mohammed ANSAR was asking, on Twitter, whether it was fitting for Parliament to make laws about what women should wear.

Mr ANSAR's name seems to be unpopular with some of my friends, and himself has certainly no reason to like me or even to know me – but this is not the time nor place for socialising...

This is a good question, well put.

The idea of passing law to forbid or impose any kind of apparel is ludicrous; it infringes the rights of the individual; it is un-effective and counter-productive.

It is a ludicrous idea – because if we look back upon the history of clothing in the last decades, we find that the segment of public opinion that has become incensed by the use of veils by certain ladies is the same that opposed short skirts, trousers for women, and going out without a hat or bonnet.

It infringes the most basic right of the individual: No state can force a person to show – or not to show – any part of her (or his) body. Except for security reasons or medical reasons, which are limited in space and time. The reason invoked to wear a veil being modesty, and modesty being not to this day an immoral purpose, one should be – and I am – most shocked by the proposal of passing law on this matter. I have opposed it in France on the same grounds. Surely it is always possible to have a security officer or health officer of the same gender as the person involved, proceed with courtesy to any necessary and legitimate investigation.

Such a law could not be properly enforced – not on this planet on the move, not in this age of extensive travel – It would expose an honest, hard-working police officer to the risk of raising diplomatic hell if some distinguished visitor happened to shop on Bond Street dressed as she would be dressed in her country.

Finally, it would run against its very purpose, because it is well known that forbidding something makes it more desirable. A friend pointed out recently that more and more young women tend to adopt the style of dressing usually linked to the East. Some of them, surely, out of conviction. Some of them, probably, because it is a way for them of thumbing a polite nose to an invasive State.

And this has nothing to do with woman's status, equality of rights, or dignity. Royal Persons in this country have been known to wear a scarf on their head. And I heard once – in a dominantly male convention – an Iranian lady, member of the Iranian parliament, deliver a most forceful speech about her country's policy. Believe me, she was no humiliated female. And, despite the chaste veils she wore, no man could ignore that she was a very gracious and seductive – woman.

19

ANIM-HALAL

9th March

I care for animals. Wanton cruelty to them should be punished in my view with the same laws as cruelty to defenceless people. But I shall become an "animal rights activists" only when there is no more reason to be a "human rights activists". I think it is obscene to mobilise to save foxes when men are sent to die or be mangled for a trumped-up cause. Even if it is "trendy". Now it is "trendy" to attack "halal" food (not only meat, mark...) because halal slaughtering is supposed to be more cruel than the modern techniques. Meaning that it is distasteful to squeamish eyes. Until recent times in Europe there has not been another way of killing a pig than by bleeding it. Courts and news media know of so many scandals in the "western-style" slaughterhouse that the argument does not hold water.

The "animal-rights" angle against halal is nothing but a hasty whitewashing of xenophobic hate. The people who antagonise halal only do it because they are afraid of Muslims. Another argument against halal food is that its proceeds might be used to finance terrorism. I do not know, but it may be true that some of the proceeds of the food chain be diverted to illicit purposes. There are however so many cases of dishonesty, fraud and extortion, that it is hard to believe that such an obvious type of business would be the only one to finance "terrorism". It is well known that some of the strongest terrorism organisations have been encouraged, funded and trained by great nations. The "terrorist-funding" angle against halal is just another whitewashing of xenophobic hate. The reality is that, by being aggressive and offensive to the majority of Muslims who keep "halal" - the hate-mongers increase their level of uncertainty, diffidence and frustration. In fact they prepare the ground for extremist preachers to recruit and inspire terrorists.

This is common sense. Hate is madness. Madness posing as "animal-right-activism" or "anti-terrorism". The irresponsible morons who call at "boycotting halal" are just that: irresponsible morons, full of hate and prejudice. Those who are tempted to follow them - all good people, ill-informed, should take every occasion to meet their neighbours - appreciate them - and move onwards to mutual understanding - and living together in peace.

20

GOD DAMN YOU ALL, MERRY GENTLEMEN

11th March 2014

I am not a gentleman. First, I am not British. Second, I come not from the upperising classes.

My forebears were peasants. True yokels, not "agricultural entrepreneurs". Dad (great guy) was a draughtsman and an surveyor. Mom (great woman) was a typist. They emigrated from Europe in 1936. Emigrated, mind you. Not expatriated. Wanted to get out to build something better for the kids to come. (I was the kid, bad luck to them). Eventually they came back to where they had come from - one of History's bad tricks... and I came too. So, I feel a double migrant: migrant, son of migrants... All right, here half of my friends go away. Fare them well.

I watch intensely what's going on in England with the Moslem population. None of my business? I love England where I have been a happy teenager. I have high regard for the Moslems among whom I have lived part of my life, and still have many friend. So you're welcome to bash me as a meddlesome ungentlemanly frog. But here I am. To stay. To talk. If necessary to fight.

I try to look at all sides.

On one side I see: working and striving communities, not prepared to live together, and thrown together in hard times: an economic crisis and an explosive demographic growth.

On the other side I see well-groomed pundits, often self-appointed, splitting the hairs of centuries-old theology and making elaborate constructions to explain why people are different and must stay different. I see politicians who from poll to poll seek re-election and make constant use of fear to twist the citizen's ballot towards their camp. Those are the merry gentlemen I address. Suggest they stuff their college ties wherever they like. Stop talking about theology and ideology (sounds like a Gilbert and Sullivan rhyme, my dear...) and roll-up their sleeves. Bring people together instead of giving them reasons to be divided.

To the working people, whose difficulties are visible to anyone that is not a pundit, a politician, or a gentleman, I say: get together. Open your doors. Open your hands. Don't listen to the hate-mongers, hate-peddlers, hate-preachers. Not easy? Sure... nothing is easy except smooth talking and being interviewed by TV.

Yes I am a foreigner, yes I am a senior officer in my country's army, yes I hold degrees, yes I have written and published books in three languages. But the one thing I want is to remain a man to the end of my life. And it's my crowd I want to help, even if they are rough and ill-informed, not the pundits and politicians that I know.

I think someone has made a decisive step towards some sort of dialogue, a working class lad, not your sort of people, Lady Millicent. I support that lad and his mates, and their counterparts, more similar in depth than dissimilar in surface. They are welcome to bash me if they don't want my help. But for the others I have but one word, and it is a rude one.

F***

21

JUSTICE: FAIR AND EQUAL?

13th March

England, the country of *habeas corpus* has always been, for me, the best and most respected example of a country where justice is dealt fairly and serenely to all. Several events in recent days have led me to deeper thoughts on the subject.

A man, committed to teaching, has been convicted of sexually assaulting a young girl while under his responsibility. He has been given a six months prison penalty- and set free for humanitarian reasons, as his wife does not speak English and could not cope with their six children. Kind and natural indeed.

This however raises the issue of prison penalties being often double-penalties, as they penalise the innocent family (spouse, children, aged parents) as well as the guilty person - and often more. Which sets the trend of an in-depth reflexion, also in France where the Minister of Justice, Christiane Taubira, has started a process of modernisation.

Some of my friends have expressed their concern that it might also raise the issue of equal treatment. One might think that six months-suspended is rather low in the scale of penalties given (even in France) for that sort of offence. Quoting the case of a man who has been given eighteen months for fraudulous misrepresentation in a mortgage case, one might suggest that in England - and probably in most "Western" countries, offences against property and money are considered graver than offences against people - or feelings. Might this be true? It would be alarming indeed.

Quoting the same case, some have suggested that a more smoothly-educated man from a higher strata of society, for instance a politician, might have got away with a far lighter sanction than this young man for a similar misdemeanour.

I have said and written, personally, that it was unfortunate to lock up this particular young man for a long time precisely when he had apparently made a move towards discussion and understanding in a very serious issue, where his former associates kindled more hate than reasonable talk - even if angry. I have also noted that no special consideration was given to the family situation of this convict.

I perfectly recall having expressed - on several social media - my opinion that such a brutal sentence of court was unfair and in my mind contemptible. Of course I may have been mistaken. But I shall not take back my words, and if they be treated as contempt of court - which in my view they should - I am quite prepared to answer for them.

22

JOUMOUHAA MOUBARAKA - BLESSED FRIDAY

14th March

Lucky Friday, or Blessed Friday, that's the usual greeting between Muslims on this day. Friday is, in Islam, the day to pray and to get-together. It is also a special day for Christians - a day of prayer and abstinence. I was brought up a Christian in a Muslim country. I know familiarly many Muslims and I deeply respect their religion and community.

This particular Friday, 21st of March is for me a day to fly back to England, talk to friends, drink beer - no worship but certainly conviviality. I am posting to-day on this blog to send greetings both to my Muslim friends and to my English friends (some of them being both, of course). With a particular thought for Tommy Robinson whose anger to the actions of some Muslims must NOT turn to hate of an entire population.

I am not young any more, I have seen considerable changes in my time. I have travelled - I have worked with many people of many countries, many ethnic origins, many philosophical orientations, many stations in life. I understand that things are not easy for people, anywhere, in a changing, globalising world, in which migrations cannot be separated from difficulties developing from economic conditions and for the various forms taken by a diffuse war, said to be against terrorism.

There are tensions everywhere - These tensions are most heavily felt by the young, by the working class, and by those that a hasty schooling has not prepared to take in their stride the changing of our world. They are vulnerable. Whatever community they belong to, they worry about their future and the future of they children. They are the great-grandsons of the men who fought the Great War - and of the women who suffered by it.

Life has taught me to see that people are pretty much the same everywhere, and that perceived differences are an illusion created and supported by fear. It has taught me also that fear could be deliberately cultivated as a formidable instrument of power, and that most ideologies are based on fear - on exciting the perception of differences. In every human community, hair-splitting pundits in the pay of some power, refine on perceived differences and increase terror, bullying the innocent and the candid into a logic of hate and war-like postures that - unfortunately, lead the weaker minded to acts of hate and war-like crimes. This must stop. Whichever community they belong to, the good men and women of this world must not become cannon-fodder or bomb-fodder to satisfy the greed of power of self-appointed elites. They must stop listening to preachers of hate and turn - simply - to their neighbours, and discover how many more reasons of feeling alike they have, than of claiming to be different. I have quoted before that "Judy O'Grady and the Colonel's lady are sisters under the skin". This is true now as ever. These two women taking their kids to the same school - one veiled, one in tight trousers - have everything in common that matters to them: the future of their kids. These two men on the same line at the Job Center - Mahmud and Tommy - are not worrying about the fine print in God's messages to Mankind. They are worrying about getting that job and the pay-check that goes with it.

The poet Shelley said "THE SOUL'S JOY LIES IN DOING". In DOING, mark, not in TALKING, PREACHING, SHOUTING, HATING...

Right... that applies to me also. Have a nice Friday, all of you...

23

BOOKS AND PRISONERS

Wednesday, 26 March 2014

Prisoners in the UK may not be sent books. When I first read that I thought it was a malevolent hoax. I perfectly accept that some filtering should be done, that and books susceptible of leading to propaganda or violence should not be admitted.

I did not share the anger of popular novelists losing a captive audience (never would the term be more appropriate). My books are in French. The one I have published in English, "The Singapore Cane" is certainly not proper for prison reading. I wondered, however, at total interdiction. I researched a little, and found that access to books and the gym were used as part of an incentive/reward system for disciplining the inmates, as well as receiving certain amenities from families and friends outside. This is wrong, in my mind. Moreover, these new rules seem to imply that the incentive/reward system escapes the authority of the Governors and directors themselves, being operated from the Ministry. This I do not believe to be in the best interest of anyone.

 I believe the operative chain of the Prison system has already expressed that to the Minister. So I shall not expatiate, but suggest their advice should be heard... I have never been in prison - yet - . But I believe it has a double purpose of punishing and rehabilitating.

I can understand that a system of incentives may be used: mails, visitors, furloughs... But books and the Gym are essential instruments for a man to gather physical and mental energy, not only to bear with present hardships, but to prepare for his return to freedom. They are not only "amenities", they imply some effort – and it is not good correction policy to raise obstacles for prisoners to reading a book or sweating in the gym. I

f prisoners cannot be sent books, as prison libraries may be threatened by funding difficulties of local authorities, this is a serious issue. I am sure that the tradition of English pragmatism will prevail and that the incentive/reward system will be sparingly implemented so that prisoners come out of prison out better men than they went in - not worse ones. [2] [3]

---

[2] My letter to the Governor of HMP Winchester got a very courteous and very firm answer from the Head of Reducing Reoffending: It appears that prison librarians have no power

24

CALLING NAMES NEVER HELPS

27th March

Amazing times! The third Reich has disappeared almost 70 years ago. Stalin died about 60 years ago.

---

to acquire, choose, or vet books, as their library provisions are contracted to County Council Library Service. I must say I find this answer very unsatisfactory. It implies that councils – as political bodies – control entirely the readings of prisoners. In any country but Great Britain, this would suggest a threat of thought supervision. At the same time, I have learnt that in Italy, prisoners are under incentive to read books, and get rewarded when they have effectively read a certain quota of pages. Prison is rightly designed to punish. But if it does not tend also to rehabilitate the offender, I believe an important point is missed out.

[3] It seems policy has been reversed – or mitigated. If it be true, it would be excellent news – for the future

The wall of Berlin was hacked down about 25 years ago. People happily too young to have known the reality of those times gleefully trade insults that obviously they don't understand.

All over Europe we have people shouting angrily at each other words that are meant as insults, resented as provocations. Words now meaningless goad men who have only known peace in their time to fight each other, for the benefit of a few major News channels. I know I am not going to turn the tide by myself. But I'd like to make a few things as clear as possible... Words are, after all, my craft.

Fascist is someone involved in a totalitarian regime based on a single party, the cult of a Chief, and paramilitary organisations for the enjoyment of people who like young males parading in shorts.

A totalitarian regime is one where the State is involved into every single step of life.

Communism is a party advocating freedom and supporting totalitarianism. Stalinism was a clever blend of Communism and Fascism. Indeed very close to Nazism

.Nazism is a fascist regime based on a supremacist ideology, and the physical annihilation of every person not conforming to the collective standards.

Supremacism is considering that one's kith and kin are necessarily better than the neighbour's, that some bloods be bloodier than others, that God (whatever be His name) has given by deed poll the rights to rule to some lost tribe and their descendants.

Neo-nazis are morons who display fetishes of Nazi Germany and get sexual boost from their sick imagination.

Now if I look around me, I see many countries tempted by totalitarianism for "efficiency's" sake. That goes for the nucleus of EU including UK... I see neo-Nazis in France, in the Netherlands, in Germany, in Austria, I see threats of fascism. Communism as I knew it in my youth is now a myth.

Nazism, emulated in its main dimension of supremacism and annihilation of the resisting few, I can only see, in some extreme dogmatic and literal fractions of Islam. over-hyped by the press, and no more representative of the Muslim masses than a mad parson in Florida can be seen to represent Christianity.

Now let us stop calling each other names, which is just a means to escape tackling reality. Reality is people, families, workers, -idlers too- literati and illiterate, good and bad people together. Reality is neighbours confronted to the same neighbourhood difficulties, reality is the common struggle for a better life in a world that gets every day more difficult to understand.

Let us all "go real". And not divert our energies to ideological or theological wars, manipulated by unscrupulous leaders who ill disguise their only motivation: the   craving   for   power.

If a community - whichever - is under pressure from unscrupulous organisations, let the adjoining communities help them to resist the pressure. That will be much better than tagging the whole community with the sin of their oppressors.

I believe it is the only way out. It is also the most dangerous. It can in some ways be compared to combat against criminal organisations in Southern Italy or the USA. It takes courage, lucidity and patience. I believe this is the way that Tommy Robinson has begun to follow - with his partners from Quilliam - with, I hope, ALL of us who support him.

25

"NO MORE MOSQUES"? NO! "MORE MOSQUES"

I have seen recently a poster displaying "no more mosques". We have the same sort of idiotic propaganda in France. Please take a moment to think, my friends... You know, that strange exercise people do with their brains.

What is a mosque? It is a place for prayer, for study, for charity. Why should their existence be offensive? There are people who need to pray, to get together to study and share. Why should they be denied a place to do it? Do you want to push them back to pray in the streets and gather in garages and derelict buildings? Why? Oh yeah... you think evil preachers might use prayer time and study time to inflame hate and destroy the fundaments of your life. But surely they can do it even better in cellars, garages, and clandestine gatherings. Pushing them back into clandestinity only gives them one more argument for hating you back.

Some complain that churches are closing as mosques are opening. Surely the Muslims are not responsible for that, but rather the Christians. Or not?

Some object that minarets break the traditional skyline of English towns. Do they? More than those splendid skyscrapers that are the pride of our metropolis?

I was forgetting... the five-times-a-day call to prayer from a muezzin whose voice is not always melodious... Not very audible during the buzz of working hours, I agree it may be disturbing in the depth of night. I could say that when I am in a Moslem country I only hear it on the first night. But you might say I am prejudiced (and you are welcome to say worse: I don't mince my words either...). No, this is a problem. To be solved in each town, between those in charge of the mosque and the local authorities. Discussion, not regulation, is needed.

Anyhow, the slogan "no more mosques" is moronic and offensive. It only pushes the honest, God-fearing community into the arms of hate-mongers. Which is the exact opposite of what should be done.

&

26

ONE GOD - AND NO QUIBBLING

29th March

One of the trickiest points in friendly conversation between a Muslim and a Christian arises right from the start, when someone invokes the Almighty.

The semantic fact that the word designating a Unique Creator - or Architect - of the Universe has no plural in Arabic, and has a plural in all the languages of the Christianised sphere - however secularised. DieuX, GodS, GöttER, DiosES, create a confusion that leads to the accusation of polytheism, as the very word Allah encompasses the idea of unicity.

This comes from our History, and from the fact that Monotheism has been imported into the languages of formerly polytheist cultures.

Man probably started as an awkward naked animal, stumbling against everything in creation; cautiously and wisely he respected - and divinised - whatever might hurt him - or protect him. (Sorry about "him", it was "her" quite as much). From pantheism: any rock being a deity by itself, the self-designated logical mind of man derived polytheism: one deity for all rocks, another for all plants, that sort of thing. As man became more conceited (yes, and woman too - or not?) he figured out that these deities should have some human, or even superhuman appearance. This takes us straight to Walhalla or Olympus, and the gloriously funny battles of gods and goddesses filling up our imagination from Homer to Offenbach and from the old Germanic lore to Wagner.

Now people living in the desert were overwhelmed by a sense of unity. T.E.Lawrence's Seven Pillars of Wisdom give beautiful accounts of that impression. It was thus natural that some shepherds' tribe, somewhere between Egypt and Mesopotamia, might have the first revelation of a unique agency responsible for creation - and what came next. Monotheism did not "name" this unique agency. The ancient Hebrews used periphrases and metaphors. The Muslims have this marvellous phrase: "He can be named by any name, though some names are preferred... and His real name will only be revealed at the End".

Christianity was born in Palestine, first as a variation of Judaism. Monotheism in a monotheistic culture. To export it northwards, its first leaders had the message translated into the language with the largest diffusion. To-day, it would probably be Anglo-American. At that time it was Greek, and then Latin. Polytheistic cultures. The translators did not see the trap they were falling into. They used the Deus/Theos word, just capitalising it to signify singularity. But as the same word - without capitals - never disappeared from our rhetoric's, we are still wide open to question about the quintessential monotheism of Christianity.

The problem arises again with the complicated dogmas of Trinity - but that is theological hair-splitting and much above and outside my province. One thing remains - and I believe that all exchange between Muslims and Christians may start from it — a principle that both these awesome communities share between them - and with the original Jews, and that is: "We believe in One creator of all visible and invisible things - who has spoken through the Prophets".

How can we seriously use Faith arguments to antagonise each other, if we accept this?

27

ISLAMISM AND NAZISM

3rd April

I am ready to fight in anger. I refuse to trade in hatred.

I do not believe in any kind of collective supremacy - be it racial or religious -

I do not believe that any family, tribe, nation or country has ever passed an exclusive agreement with God.

I respect the religion of those who feel the need for a structural relationship to their idea of God.

I respect the atheism of those who feel no need for an idea of God.

I do believe that all human beings have equal rights.

I do not believe in sin, original or individual. I believe in responsibility of everyone towards the others - and towards himself. - at a price, not in the next world but in this.

I believe in human justice and retribution, that any community has a right to establish its rules of law and order, according to its customs and the will of its citizens.

I like to believe that all communities might be organised into one. But I am not THAT candid...

Most of the fore-mentioned points would condemn me to be put to death by a Nazi state. Add to them the fact that I am homosexual. That, I expect, clears me of any possible charge of weakness to the neo-Nazis.

Some men in Europe, who have NOT known the times of Nazism, entertain a vague nostalgia of something they certainly do not understand. Some of them are actual psychological cases that may commit terrible crimes. Most content themselves with parading in grotesque attire, collecting memorabilia and chanting offensive songs. I dislike them, because they are parrots repeating words of hate that can only produce new hate. I find they are troublesome. I do not believe them to be more than individually or occasionally dangerous. There is, however, a new danger coming, similar to Nazism, but far more powerful, and far more capable of extending to the entire planet - leading to the destruction of mankind as we share it.

It is not neo-Nazism. It is Political Islamism.

Nazism was founded on the supremacy of an imaginary Aryan race and planned the annihilation of all those who did not conform to the standard of their party. Race supremacy is nowadays difficult to support. But Islamism is founded on the supremacy of a Faith. A learned man called Sayyid Qutb, a member of the Muslim Brotherhood, who was executed in 1966, has expounded, in a small book called "MILESTONES", a theory of political takeover of the world, under the supremacy of Islam as he read it, Shall I quote? :"*The people who are really chosen by God are the Muslim community which has gathered under God's banner without regard to differences of races, nations, colours and countries*" or "*The Islamic society is, by its very nature, the only civilised society, and the* jahili *societies, in all their various forms, are backward societies.*" Such a totalitarian vision, exclusive of any other kind of reference than submission, is clearly a terrible threat to the billions of people who do not follow Islam. It is no use saying that "this is ideology" and "it must be separated from radical activism", because the history of Nazism gives ample proof that ideology always finds activists to carry on its programme. A Hitler and a Rosenberg always find Roehm's and Heydrich's to implement their criminal concepts.

The equivalent for our days of the Nazi threat, as it was known or ignored in the 1930s, is the Islamist threat, as represented by doctrinaire groups who claim religious and ideological supremacy for themselves.

This does not imply of course that all Muslims must be considered as possible Islamists. As all the Germans in 1934 were far from being Nazis. Yet between 1940 and 1945 - and afterwards... it was all the German people that suffered from association to the Nazis. It is a prime necessity to SAVE the Muslims from Islamism. In the Middle East, as well as in the heart of London or Paris. How to do it is certainly not to mouth indiscriminate hate, but rather, by proximity actions, ease the fear on both sides, and **get people talking**. Not theologians or politicians to confuse issues, but people, talking about everyday life. People becoming conscious of the threat and willing to rise in anger against it. And demanding that Justice be unprejudiced, fair, and intransigent.

28

TURNING THE TIDE OF VIOLENCE

11th April

Twitter is a fantastic meeting place. Out of thousands of shallow contacts, suddenly may spring an unexpected and authentic friendship, and in a maze of useless information one may find a surprising gem. This is how I met an Algerian writer named Maamar Rekaiba, who writes in French, about his country, a colony of France for almost one and half century, that became independent fifty years ago, after a long and bitter war whose scars are far from healed to-day. His books, written with a very precise pen, tell of the years that followed independence, the country led by the dictatorship of a Marxist-oriented party, then torn by a civil war easily labelled in Europe as "Islamic terror".

I was enthralled by his account of disorder, of cruelty, of corruption, of the sly meddling of foreign powers, but also by the great humanity of his picture of a people so much like the Moroccan people I know better, a generous and friendly people, of men ready to fight for their kin, of proud women standing fast against adversity. One book, in particular, fascinated me: called "La Décrue" (the ebbing of a river flood) it tells the story of a man trapped into a resistance movement, who gets to question the real purpose of his gruesome warfare, and turns the tide of violence, restoring peace around him and in his own wounded heart.

At the same time, on Twitter also, I had made some younger English friends, very loud and angry. Anger is of course in the nature of young men, but their anger some people consider dangerous. Our world changes. Our old countries perhaps feel the change most, and feel it ruefully. Social, economic and demographic pressure on one side, cultural differences on another, make it more difficult for growing communities to live through their differences. The wars carried on in distant territories cannot but affect the feelings of people who migrated from these places towards our countries. This makes a perfect breeding ground for unscrupulous politicians and professional agitators. My young friends were loyal to their camp, and their anger, stirred by dramatic events, was on the point of turning to hate.

Reading "La Décrue" I realised then that I wanted them to read this book. About a young man so full of anger that he becomes an actor of the worst possible violence, until he pauses and reflects. It was easier to translate the book than to teach them French... so... the book is just out. It is called "TAMING THE RIVER" by Maamar REKAIBA. It contains a very vivid account of the fake hateful preachers, who by carefully selecting words out of the enormous religious literature of Islam, drive people into the spiral of terror.

It is obvious that the principal victims of these men are their own people.

It is certain that the best way to turn the tide is not to play their games, and enter into theological contests with them, but to prevent them from bullying those who live around them, and so stop the spiral of hate.

I do not know if I shall convince all my young English friends... I believe one of them might be capable to work out a way out of hate. I believe Tommy Robinson could do it, if he wanted.

I translated this book for him and his friends - and for the young Muslims of England, who might be tempted by those preachers of evil.

Who knows? It may work... InshaAllah!!!

29

PEOPLE MATTER, NOT WORDS

12th April

So few people read my blog - why should I lose my time writing in it? Words do not matter. People matter. Talking to people. Smiling to people. Sharing with people the troubles of modern life, the nostalgia of imaginary pasts, the anguishes of a dark future - Sharing salt and bread, fruit and milk, worry about education and jobs for the children. Never mind colour, creed or language. People are people.

Every community has their share of black sheep - with or without a beard - with or without a taste for violence or for destructive speeches.

Do not see the fold black because of some sheep...

Fight political Islamism - you'll find me on your side

Fight for the greatness and future of your country - you'll find me on your side

Respect Muslims and migrants - you'll find me on your side

Respect the flag, the laws, the symbols of Britain, her institutions and her army - you'll find me on your side

Focus your anger on facts, not ideas -you'll find me on your side

Hang on to the old fumes of white supremacism, you'll find me against you.

Feed your hate on daydreams, -you'll find me against you.

Turn your hate on millions of innocent people, - you'll find me against you

Aim at destroying the country you live in - you'll find me against you

Let oxbridgian or would-be pundits coax you into confusing theological debate - you'll find me against you.

Because generalised hate just pushes the innocent under the oppression of the evil

Because any violence that goes in the wrong direction of bullying people will eventually benefit to political Islamism.

Political Islamism is evil. It is Nazism cloaked under the mantle of religion. Crafty evil preachers can pick out of any book words that can be used to purposes of hate and death. Let us not fall into that trap.

More than ideologies, politics, doctrines, religious dogma, people are what matters. All those constructions of the mind have no other purpose than to make people live together, more or less peacefully, more or less happily.

Respect the other person for their existence, their work, their love, their qualities - don't despise or hate them for being different from you.

30

SCARING PEOPLE

14th April

Fear, Fright, Scare, Terror… This is what affects people and leads them down the path of hate and self-destruction. There may even be no real cause to panic, but the mere suspicion or imagination of danger. A flock of sheep will rush down a cliff if raced by a dog with only playful intentions. So of people.

We are animals, thank God, and, thank God again, we have a large brain and the liberty to choose our way. The complex working of our larger brain may be used at our free will either for enhancing the capabilities of our animal nature, or for limiting them into the frame of the communities we build.

Thus, we may let our predatory instinct veer towards crime, or we may curb it into the formalities of justice.

Thus, we can master our fear and turn it to cautious curiosity, or we can unshackle it and be carried away into panic.

As we are a social animal, living in man-made communities much more complex than the original pack of wolves or fold of sheep, an individual's attitude to fear will take a greater importance if that individual is in a position to influence a greater number of other individuals. Those who exploit the fear of others, use it to increase their power or to force the community into a direction that would not naturally be chosen, as contrary to the basic vital interest of all, those I call terrorists.

The strangely accoutred man who vows death to those who do not agree with him is a terrorist.

The well-dressed man who announces Doomsday to those who do not vote for him is also a terrorist.

Both, in their way, are using fear to promote their ideas or their interests, They scare others to impose their mad certainty of being right.

And people are easily scared.

31

FEAR OF CHANGE

15th April

A young friend of mine, hefty and loud in his English patriotism, shrugged off his disapproval of my views telling me that I should understand that the England I knew in the 1950's is no more...

Who did he think I was? Rip van Winkle, Robinson Crusoe?

Of course England has changed. I have seen it change. The world has changed and goes on changing fast.

Yeah, said my friend, but it has changed for the worse.

What the fuck! It is not a matter of good vs evil. Change is not good or bad: it is indifferent. It happens, that's all. One may have a nostalgia for the smell of toast burning on a fire of coke, yet use the latest electronic toaster... The parameters of social life, national life, and the world, are so many and so complex, that change is not really a matter of choice. Economy, science, technical skills, and the universal desire of people for freedom, happiness, and an easier life, those are the factors of change, and people who stand out as actors are more coincidental or accidental than they would like to admit.

Change is not the issue. The problem is how we react to change. Change disturbs us and frightens us. This is deep into our animal nature. A gust of wind, a whiff of smell, a twig crackling, and the animal is on alert, ready to flee - or to attack. All animals are conservative. But animals are deprived of that large brain and capacity to decide that are God's gifts to us - or the result of evolution if you will.

What that large brain tells us is that all clouds have a silver lining and that, to the contrary, all blessings may be mixed. Our world is changing fast because of a general increase of population, a growing need for energy, a modification of the climate, a greater mobility of persons and goods, and a global system of communication and sharing of information.

No country can escape this world change. No country can revert to splendid isolation. Politicians who advocate this are fools or liars or both.

So?

The world is changing. England is changing. Change started with the world creation and will go on to the end. Change scares people. It has always done so. Change is like the wind, erratic, sometimes mild and sometimes wild. One does not stop the wind. One does not shout at the wind. What one can do, and must do, is to set one's own course to take advantage of it, and make sure it will not capsize the family boat.

The winds of change, my hefty patriotic young friend, are neither good nor bad. It's up to you to turn them to your advantage, and set up your sails to go your own English way. And the English way, which will never change, is to keep calm during a storm.

32

WHAT THE F***?

What the hell!

I respect everyone and every opinion - I try to observe and understand using my experience not as Revealed Truth but as a means to get closer to the truth - In spite of my visceral revulsion to racism and xenophobia I have listened to the drivel of far-right extremists in my country - France - and in a country I love - England - I do sympathise with the plight of people bewildered by changes that they believe politicians could and would control. But now I have had enough.

I see the danger of totalitarian political Islamism rising. Perhaps I see it even more clearly and more apprehensively than those noisy Islamophobes do, as this totalitarian global state is much closer to their own vision. I recognise in it the features of Nazism, of Stalinism, under the guise of Islamism.

I know Muslim people - good people - quiet people - with the same desires and the same aspiration to peace as the rest of the world. I know that a totalitarian Islamic state is NOT what they desire.

I suggest that blind, insulting hostility to all Muslims can have only one result: to push the timid ones towards the mad extremist preachers leading towards ever greater confrontation, ever more violence, ever more hate.

I say: Fight Political Islamism - Respect all Muslims.

All I get back is insults or jeering remarks.

Enough is enough.

33

THANK YOU, MR SMITH

18th April

There is a man (I should call him a gentleman but will not) by the name of Smith who has got really angry at my - usually bland enough - words. I want to thank him.

Not for his insults: they don't touch me: as we say in France "the frog's spittle does not touch the white feathers of the dove"

I thank him for goading me into NOT stopping my blog and into opening it to comments. Any comments. Including those of "Mr Smith".

I am up again and fighting. Fighting for people to live with their neighbours and try to understand each other.

Is that utopia and madness? Put me in bedlam.

Is that treachery? Shoot me.

All I say is this: people who peddle hate and violence are criminals. They are more responsible for terrorism than the rank-and-file people who kill and get killed.

If I were in London to-day, I'd be in the demo against Anjem Choudary.

Not only to free my environment from a dangerous maniac, but to free the Muslims from one dangerous bully.

There should be demos also against people like "Mr Smith" (expect his real name be Jones or Shittypond) because they are dangerous bully and demagogues.

And I'd like to be there too.

Because political agitators are the same - whatever the creed they use as a weapon. Criminal perverts who drive honest young men to killing and death for their own ideological gratification.

Unfortunately, fighters also are all the same. Young people with a yearning to a beautiful and glorious world and letting themselves be driven into a world of hate and violence. They are all the same. The camp they are in depends on their background - and on the first evil preacher or agitator they come up with.

A brave young man will end up indifferently in Nazi-like hooliganism or in Jihad. It's up to us to save him from both violences. Question motives. Jail major offenders. Talk of peace not of war. Put foul-mouth speakers away from their audience.

And that includes you, Mister Smith. Screw you.

34

FEAR ON THE MARKETPLACE

19th April

I was on the town market this morning. About one half of the stands are held by immigrants, mosly North-African Muslims. About one third of the shoppers are Africans (Northern or Central). I am always shocked by the black looks exchanged between people. To say the least, they show indifference. To say the most, they glare hostility and fear. Local old ladies with pursed-up mouths, scornful men, aggressive youths, on both sides.

Now if you succeed in meeting one pair of eyes and giving a slight nod, everything changes. You get a not of recognition. When I get down the pavement to leave room for two veiled ladies with parcels and prams, I get a guarded smile. So what? Just being polite in my town, on my market place, with other people who come here for the same reason as I.

All this indifference and hostility comes from fear. People are afraid of those who are different, of those who look different, whom they expect to act different. But there is no difference. Watch these two women buying apples or lettuce. They have the same gestures, they play the same game of getting the best for less...

They are different. One was born sixty years ago, not one mile from here. The other was born thirty years ago, two thousand miles from here. They are alike: women buying food on the Saturday morning market.

The great reason for hostility is fear. Mutual fear. Animal fear. Dogs bare their teeth and bark at other dogs only because there is fear between them. People and animals don't like to be disturbed in their mental routine. Anything and anyone different is seen as a threat.

We are reasonable creatures, are we not? Forget the threat. Forget the fear. Forget the difference. Be kind to whomever is your neighbour.

And let us all get out of this vicious circle of hatred.

35

RESPECT THE SOLDIER

20th April

A French writer of the XVIIIth century, who had been an officer in the Army, VAUVENARGUES, wrote this: "*le vice fomente la guerre, la vertu combat*" - " vice stirs up the wars, virtue fights them" - and he added: "*s'il n'y avait aucune vertu, nous aurions pour toujours la paix*" - "were there no virtue left, we should live for ever in peace".

This is the idea that comes to my mind whenever I think of those men and women who dedicate themselves to a cause, to the extent that they accept to die for it - and to kill for it. All the Tommy Atkinses of this world so easily forgotten until the drums begin to roll. It takes virtue to go out and fight. The cause of the fight may escape the fighter -

nay, it always escapes him. History may even declare it to have been unjust. Does it matter?

Of course, it matters to the citizen, to the historian, to the politician, to those who watch the fight from the comfort of their library, armchair, or seat in Parliament. For the latter, it is all important to show that the war they declared is a just one. That Saddam Hussein HAD weapons for massive destruction. This is what Vauvenargues called vice.

The fighter goes forth on an impulse of what seems right to him. Be it a flag, an idea, a religion, essentially loyalty to one's family, to one's friends, to one's conscience. Does it matter that it be an illusion? It matters to the newspaper who will whisk up public opinion into a cloud of glory or a mist of pain. For the fighter himself it is no illusion. It is duty. And loyalty. What Vauvenargues called virtue.

This is why I have been shocked by most comments about the death in Syria of a young man from Brighton. He went there out of loyalty to a relative whom he felt had been badly treated at Guantanamo. He went there on an illusion. He died for it. He must be respected. His father called him a martyr. That also must be respected: indeed he was made a martyr by those who caused the war to happen - and caused him to go fight it.

The leaders of several sides who have unleashed Al Qaeda in Syria and in other countries - under various fallacious pretexts, the loud and pervert preachers in London or elsewhere who have indoctrinated young men to comply with their evil schemes, those are what Vauvenargues called vice. Those must be fought, and despised, and stopped, and punished, and destroyed.

Make no mistake: All soldiers, in or out of uniform, whatever their flag or creed, all soldiers are like Tommy Atkins. Respect to them.

36

FIGHTING FOR A CAUSE

21st April

The urge to fight is, I believe, deeply embedded in the nature of man.

Animals fight for a territory - for the possession of a female - for physical supremacy - they fight to survive.

Man has not changed much in that respect: it is just that social life has put a veneer upon the fighting instinct: Lawyers, sporting fields, and the resources of economy and medicine make it less obvious - and less necessary; divorce courts and football games are vastly preferred to duels, and survival depends more on NHS and food stamps than on grabbing the other man's prey. As a rule, I mean.... There are cases.

One of the great inventions of man is fighting for an

abstract cause. Class rights, Political rights, Social rights, "Freedom", "Democracy", or the greatest of all abstractions: "God". Those abstract causes have proved much more deadly than the former elementary instinctive causes, yet they are considered nobler, more "human". Precisely because man has founded his supremacy on some abstraction he calls "intelligence" and believes it is more intelligent to bomb a city or send a drone upon a house that to go out and chin the man next door.

This might take some discussion. But there it is. Man feels the urge to fight for a cause.

For some reason, man is also equipped with a sense of guilt. Whether it has always been there or it has been progressively imbedded by priests, shamans, gurus, rabbis, imams, doctors, pundits, whatever... might also take some discussion. But there it is. Man wants to believe in the justice of its cause.

Each individual Catholic, Protestant, Revolutionary, Counter-Revolutionary, Socialist, Nihilist, Communist, Fascist, Islamist, believes in the justice of his cause - and he is ready to fight for it. If he has any balls.

Now causes are collective movements, springing from obscure depth and developed by "leaders" whose urge is not to fight, but to lead. The justice of a cause depends much of the angle under which it is observed. History teaches us that the brightest clouds may reveal in time a dark lining. Young men who went enthusiastically to fight in Catalonia found themselves embroiled with the Stalinists. Others who seriously believed in a splendid Gothic Millennium became accomplices to the gas chambers horror of Hitler.

It is usually the young who fight. Why do they espouse a cause? Certainly not out of mature reflection: they are not mature and reflection usually leads to cowardice - or peace-loving to put it mildly.

Often they follow the trend of their environment. Comparing the first pages of Maajid Nawaz' great book "Radical" with an interview I have seen of Tommy Robinson, I was astonished at the SIMILARITY of their experiences. "Paki" vs "Geordie" - I believe that if they had been born in opposite families, Tommy might well have gone to Egypt and Maajid founded EDL

Young men never listen to their fathers, but pick for themselves an heroic father-figure or big-brother-figure cut out for their admiration and imitation. So...do you not see what I am driving at? We have young men who go astray, put a towel around their head and let themselves be led to the battlefields of Syria by unscrupulous leaders. The oversimplified ideas propagated by those leaders, the dramatization of the example of men who trod the same path before, have a fatal attraction on the young. Not because they are "bad", but because they are young, and usually because they are "good". Because fighting - any sort of fighting - is better than resignation and submission.

Of course they constitute a danger, not only to themselves and their families, but to our society from which they sprang and to which they belong. How can we save them - and save ourselves? Certainly not by jailing them as soon as they come back, giving them - at a price - an aura of glory. They want a cause? They want heroes?

Well, let us give them a decent cause. Let us give them decent heroes. Let us give them Europe. Not the timid European Union of trivial petty regulations interfering with the will of the people. Not the fat European Union of greedy bankers. A great confederation of free Nations with a common past and common interest in the future. There is much to build,

Let us give them the great men and women of Europe. Not be-whiskered figures of the distant past, not glamorous blingy silhouettes of Prime Time, but the real heroes: scientists, athletes, technicians, artists, people who have really broken through a limit to knowledge and craft and strength.

If we look at ourselves. If we look at the spectacle our world offers, we may, I think, understand if not excuse, young men who feel outraged and rush out to fight. Any fight.

37

FATHER OF LIES

22nd April

Satan, Iblis, whatever... Of all the names given to the Devil - the one I find most adequate is that of FATHER OF LIES. Because all evil in Mankind rests on the exploitation of lies, misinformation, misunderstanding, and carefully nurtured ignorance.

Confusing issues, amalgamating and generalising partial truths is the easy way most lies are crafted. There are so many instances!!! Fighting those easy generalisations is as impossible as Hercules' task of cutting all the heads of the Hydra, or Don Quixote's fantasy of fencing off the windmills.

Those lies are purposely constructed to stir up hate and violence, build up individual or collective selfishness and distrust, prevent people to realise that they are but one - and that, if they believe in one God, it stands to reason that it is the same One...

No, all Muslims do **not** all read in the teaching of their Book the imperative of violence that many Islamist political activists use for their own purposes.

No, all the money shared by Muslims in their Charities does **not** fatally end in buying arms and financing terrorism.

No, all the Muslims in Britain do **not** aspire to establishing sharia in the shires, and cut off hands and stone adulterers... On the contrary: most Muslims in Britain aspire to live as Britons, most Muslim charities apply one of the fundaments of Islam: sharing wealth with the destitute, and most Muslims want to live in peace and give their children education and welfare.

No, all the British patriots are **not** ignorant, beer-swigging, hate-belching hooligans;

No, all the British patriots are **not** Nazis or neo-Nazis or Nazi-fanciers, dreaming of white supremacy.

No, all the British patriots are **not** dangerous thugs to be best kept in high security jails where they can be comfortably basted by authentic thugs. On the contrary, British patriots are honest people who want their country to be respected in its flag, in its institutions, in its soldiers, in its police force.

It is a truth that many Muslims have proven themselves - and prove themselves every day, to be British patriots. I believe **it is** also **a truth** that Britons of all creeds (or no creed) are made to live in peace together.

Only the Father of Lies can stir up contradiction between both communities, driving them to mutual hatred and violence, for the greater profit of many-coloured demagogues. You may not believe me. Then you probably believe that the war started in Iraq by George W Bush, and into which Tony Blair has let Britain be involved, was a just war to free a country from a hateful tyrant and prevent him from using existing Weapons of Mass Destruction.

It is up to you, my friends...

38

ST GEORGE AND EUROPE

23rd April

On this day of St George, I have a particular thought for a young man whom I believe to be a born chief of men and a great patriot - Tommy Robinson. I know this day is important for him and how strongly he must feel that he cannot be with his family and friends to-day.

I send my best greetings and wishes to my many English friends - and to the greater number of English people who are NOT my friends.

My salute goes to the country that has stood fast against all totalitarian attempts against Freedom and the balance of power in Europe. From the Hapsburg Holy Roman Empire to Louis XIV to Napoleon and Hitler.

Europe has been built by all of us. Europe belongs to all of us. We all belong to Europe. And that includes the United Kingdom. And that includes Britain.

It was a great mistake not to involve Britain in the initial process of European construction, because the particular insight of the British into world politics and their remarkable pragmatic attitude would have been essential. But there it is. The European Union is not perfect but it exists, and England, Britain is part of it.

In a month's time, we - all the citizens of Europe - are going to elect, democratically, a Parliament. That Parliament's job will be to promote democracy over technocracy, to take a few steps forward to making Europe the World Power it has a right to be. Electing people who do NOT believe in European construction would be, again, a terrible mistake[4].

This is a festive day and I do not wish to be a bore... And it may be said that promoting Europe on St George's Day is a bit tactless... that it is very well to do it from far away, hiding behind one's computer, but that this writer should get a deserved Agincourt salute and probably some more muscular treatment in any pub in England to-day. Save your punches, mates, and keep your fists clenched: I'll soon be back in England and you'll be free to express your feelings...

Just think of this: IF Europe had taken the necessary steps to have a common Foreign and

---

[4] Well.. I am afraid the mistake HAS been made...never mind !

Defence policy, there's no way the United Kingdom would have been lured by Bush into the catastrophic war in Iraq.

Think of it, my friends... and let us all drink to St George and England - without any moderation!

39

SUPREMACIST THREATS

24th April

I have exposed radical, political Islamist activism as similar to Nazism. I have never ceased to expose and deride its leaders as hate-mongers and enemies, not only of the "western" world, but of they own people, which I believe to be in vast majority as honest, as corrupt, as peaceful, as easily stirred, as ill-informed as any other people. The religious supremacist theory of the Muslim Brotherhood and other organisation should not be allowed to spread hate and incite to violence. Even if it is expressed in the blandest and most pious of speeches.

We must not underestimate the other side of the threat: the survival of the racial supremacist creed. It is hard to believe that, a mere lifespan after the revelation of the horrors of the Nazi methodical genocide, there should still be human beings capable of supporting such a doctrine. I have had the curiosity of following a person who sent me rather unpleasant messages via twitter, and it was as if, turning up a stone, I had found a mass of crawling maggots. Except that they are not only repulsive: they are full of hate and poison and their aggressiveness may not be limited to words.

These people are the exact counterpart of the most hateful Islamic preachers - their call is to violence and hate- their number is limited, but their underground influence is dangerous. They may oppose each other and apparently neutralise each other, but they are more rivals than adversaries, because they share the same anti-Semitism and they target a common enemy: Call it Freedom, call it Democracy, call it Equality of Rights, call it Respect of the individual, it is the deepest aspirations of mankind that these dangerous freaks want to suppress.

Let us make no mistake. The peaceful Muslim may keep a resigned silence in front of the war-mongering scum because of their inbred religious fatalism, and the peaceful Patriot may shrug off the white racist scum because of their inbred scepticism. The supremacists, however, capitalise on genuine concern and natural solidarity, and warp them into unreasonable fears and unforgivable hate.

Education, of course, is the answer. Truth, not political lies of whichever colour, must serve as a base for the future of Mankind, if we want our children to live a better life than ours, not to be enslaved by any form of totalitarian terror.

Vigilance, of course, is necessary. To help the masses to rid themselves of their evil agitators, a constant watch must be kept against propaganda and bullying. On all sides.

This is why I support Tommy Robinson, because he has had the lucidity to see how some of his own people might incline towards Nazi-like supremacism, and the courage to say that it was not to be accepted.

Because Nazism and Political Islamism are heads and tails of the same forged coin. Britain has defeated the one, not to capitulate before the other.

40

SHARIA AND MAGNA CARTA

25th April

A Moroccan student has pointed out to me a remarkable paper in "Zamane" - a extremely professional and fascinating magazine of History. The title of the article is "Morocco-England: 800 years of diplomacy" (*Zamane, #36, nov 2013, pp 84 & fol.*). I have found its content astonishing and thought-provoking.

In A.D. 1213, King John (Lackland) sent to the Almohade king of Marrakesh, Muhammad en-Nasir a trio of envoys: Knights Sir Thomas Hardington and Sir Ralph Fitz-Nicholas, and priest Robert of London. The gist of the English king's message is known by the *Chronica Majora* of Matthew Paris, a monk of St Alban's, who had it from Robert of London himself.

King John offered to pay homage to the Moroccan king, for himself and his kingdom, and embrace the Mohammedan faith, submitting himself and his subjects to the law of Islam - the *sharia*.

Even more extraordinary was the answer of Muhammad en-Nasir: It was a dry and clear rebuttal: "...*I understand that your miserable sovereign (...) wishes that his free-born subjects become slaves (...) thus he can only be the most miserable of all human beings (...)*" Muhammad en-Nasir added: "*This irresponsible apostasy brings up to my nostrils the most foetid stench ever*".

Thus thwarted in his madcap plan of submitting his country to *sharia*, King John had no issue that to accept the tryst at Runnymede and sign the *Magna Carta* – willy-nilly as is well known.

Observing as I do, in friendship and good faith, the present situation in England, I cannot but point out:

-the dignity of the Muslim monarch, - which does not surprise anyone with some knowledge or insight of Medieval Islam and of Morocco - contrasting sharply with the present base appeals to *khilafa* by irresponsible morons, preachers and terrorist agitators.

-the strange willingness of a ruler to comply with laws foreign and contrary to the rights and aspirations of his free-born people;

-the importance of that tentative submission of England in the writing of *Magna Carta,* one of the strongest foundations of the liberties and rights of the English, later an inspiration of Western democracy.

Perhaps, after all, my English friends, will the present crisis open a fantastic opportunity for the *Magna Carta* of the XXIst century... to mark the 800th anniversary of the original one! I am certain that most English Muslims will be glad to co-operate in that great work, emulating the dignity of the 13th century Almohade.

41

ABOUT PHOBIAS

26th April

Sometimes I hear young parents explain proudly that their offspring suffers from severe **spanakiophobia**, requiring both dietetical and psychological attention. I still remember how my own parents persuaded me to eat my spinach and be quick about it.

I remember also how young paratrooper recruits were apt to suffer a bout of **acrophobia** at one point of training. When peer pressure was not enough, instant cure might be achieved by a strong application of Sergeant's boot.

Things have changed a bit, and there is more respect

for the various phobias. One must say there is also an ever growing number or those phobias attacking the consciousness or unconsciousness of individuals as well as social bodies. I personally suffer from acute **anontophobia**, meaning that stupid people frighten me.

Phobias are unreasonable fears that no reason can cure. Considered as diseases of the mind, they must not lead to stigmatisation. They can be named, however, and identified, and the patients must not be put into conditions of harming themselves - or harming others.

Some phobias are individual - like **agoraphobia** and its opposite **claustrophobia**, fear of staying in the closet or fear of coming out. Not everyone gets over them easily, and they are a real danger for the people concerned, as well as a good source of profit for the psychological professions. But they are seen as just freakish individualities. **Social phobias** are much worse, because the patients tend to agglutinate and, by the sheer effect of number and collective dynamics, rush into **panic**, murderous stampede or mass suicide.

Social phobias I put under the generic term of **xenophobia** - the unreasonable, unreasoning fright of whomever is foreign to one's standards, whomever is different, in any way, from oneself, and from the standards of one's close community. It is obvious that xenophobia is strongest in those communities that feel threatened by the "invasion" of foreign elements.

When there is a large or "critical" number of foreign elements it is natural that they should develop counter-xenophobia in their own fragile community.

So we have **racism** and **anti-racism**, also **islamo-phobia, hebraicophobia, christiano-phobia, atheophobia** and, of course, **homophobia** because the most important social differences spring out of "racial" origin, "religious" background and sexual orientation.

In the countries where we have the privilege to live, these phobias are recognised as dangerous for civil peace. They have been identified as **social diseases** - We are very progressive indeed. Where we are not progressive in on dealing with these diseases. We apply therapies that were outdated long ago: Punitive therapies. **We make laws to make the disease illegal**.

Surely this is utter stupidity, Honourable Lawmakers?

When the disease cannot be cured at the source (though in many cases I believe it can be), it is important to prevent its contagious spreading with general prophylactic measures: truthful information, broad-minded education, and a general sense of purpose for the global community.

Now when the diseased person or community becomes a threat for the rest, I do not see any alternative but surgery.

Patience and understanding are necessary.

Compassion too. But any national community must recognise the danger of social phobias - whatever their nature, and deal effectively with that danger instead of toying with it to ensure electoral profit.

42

CURING A PHOBIA

29th April

Hate in words and actions springs from social phobias - be they founded on sex, race or religion.

In our densely-populated, and at the same time globally-interconnected world, it is obvious that such phobias are growing in number and strength, opening dangerous rifts in communities and kindling countless - and senseless - conflicts.

Can this disease be cured?

We need to remember how a social phobia develops in a healthy community. It starts with fear, then grows up with pointed and selected information, to become a deadly obsession. An example might be the

Germanophobia in Britain during WW1- The nation, before 1914, had no real cause of anger against Germany. Suddenly, the first months of war revealed the true dangers of a total warfare that, perhaps, had not been expected by the opinion. This brought fear. War propaganda capitalised upon this fear, distilling information about the atrocities committed in Belgium by those who became "the Hun". In a few months, this fear became a phobia that led to actions that may make us smile nowadays: the Monarch changing the dynasty's name from Saxe-Coburg to Windsor; dog-breeders renaming "Alsatian" the German shepherd-dog, and there is even an account of a dachshund being ruthlessly killed in a London street...

This was pure hate, a Germanophobia that was NECESSARY for the conduct of the war. The bloodiest, most murderous war ever. Ours not to judge but to understand. And learn.

We are witnessing now in our countries the second stage of the process: that of propaganda stirring up existing fears into phobias. To what purpose? It would take volumes to build hypotheses, and any of these might be used for propaganda in its turn. The obvious answer is: "to no purpose at all" - because wars and civil unrest never end to any party's benefit. Victory is a myth, a consolation prize to the survivors.

I believe it is still possible to turn the tide. I believe an effort CAN be successfully made to allay the basic mutual fears of co-existing communities. I believe en effort MUST be made to stop irresponsible war-mongers to propagate false and biased information.

In no case must the victims of propaganda be frightened into more hatred, by outlawing their fear instead of curing it. Because their victimisation attracts sympathy, and as small brooks turn into large rivers, Hate might soon turn mainstream. This is already obvious in the results of many elections in other countries.

It must not happen. The entire community threatened by conflicting phobias must react - Leaders must take the necessary steps to stop hate-stirring propaganda OF ANY KIND - citizens must take a deep breath, look at reality, at facts, not at news items broadcast again and again in an endless poisonous loop.

At the same time, attention must be paid to the grounds where these phobias develop. The vulnerable, fragile fringes of the national community, the people who have lost, lose or fear to lose their jobs, those who see their future threatened - or that of their children. This means housing, work, infrastructure, economy.

It means politics. Not competitive demagogy.

43

FAST FOOD AND ISLAMAFIA

1st May

My Muslim friends know that I have much respect for their religion. In this very blog, a few days ago, I stressed that *halal* food was not an issue. I believe that a technique of slaughter may be developed to conciliate animal welfare and religion. I think it is perfectly admissible, even necessary, that Muslims might find *halal* shops in their neighbourhood, as Jews *kosher* shops. I go so far as to support that institutions where individuals are in some way in the obligation of taking their meals, as barracks, schools, prisons, should provide *halal* and *kosher* food for their inmates.

But the buck stops here. If it be true that a famous chain of fast-food caterers have decided that hundreds of their shops would ONLY serve *halal* food this raises a completely different and graver issue. Firstly, one may question that decision as business policy. We are talking of a chain of franchised main-street shops catering to youngish, trendy, urban people. The majority of that *clientele* is certainly not Muslim. They are not bigot either so many of them would not care, any more than I would, if the meat was *halal* or not. However they may like a ham sandwich or a bacon roll, deeply embedded into English culture, and this decision deprives them of this choice. So they will go away. The franchise may lose a substantial percentage of their non-Muslim patronage. So it is stupid management.

So why? We do not think they could seriously establish that they act "on request of a majority of customers". Present Muslim customers have already eaten the brand's sandwiches and consequently don't care about *halal* - the request could only come from *prospective* customers.

I believe the truth is that this firm is interested in the large business opportunity offered by emerging countries with a huge youthful population, very much drawn to the so-called Western life-style. Most of these countries are Islamic. Some of them support actively militant Islam. Western businesses that want to open branches there (and will they!!!) are open to pressure.

It amounts to blackmail, by the global **ISLAMAFIA**, and forcing businesses to turn *halal* against their own local interest to be allowed to make more money in Islam-ruled land. Now why should these businesses cave in? Because they want more and more profit.

I think it was Lenin who said that capitalists would sell the very rope for communists to hang them with. This is what is happening with our greedy capitalists caving in before foreign Islamic-political pressure.

If your franchised fast-food shop really turns *halal* don't hold it against the Muslims of England - hold it against those who hold the capital and want to increase their profit at any cost.

44

TOFFS AND PLEBS

2nd May

Foreigners who believed they knew something of Britain have been flummoxed by the "plebgate" affair. That a cabinet minister might have reportedly insulted a policeman on duty calling him "pleb" reveals the persistence in British society of a form of discrimination that is most incompatible with democracy: discrimination based on social origin.

As I have been trying, all along the writing of this blog, to understand why so much hate and mutual ignorance could poison the relationship between my English friends and the muslim community in their country - myself loving everything English and respecting Islam as I have learnt to appreciate it, I have realised that this issue of social discrimination was one of the key factors of global misunderstanding.

My parents were migrants, I migrated myself back to where they had come from. I know that the main goal of people who migrate is to better their situation, breed their children in better circumstances, and adopt the higher standard of living of their new country - without losing the traditions and culture of their lifelong identity. They have no reason nor right to question the law of the land. However I hold that people who choose to live in a country have as much right to do so and be respected that those who were born there by chance and have made no effort to look elsewhere.

It is but natural that the children of immigrants strive to access the upperising classes, go to college, adopt smart dress-codes, mirroring the most respectable image of their new country. As sportsmen of former colonies have become masters in the very characteristic and baffling art of playing cricket.

Now immigrants naturally attract the attention of the ruling classes. They have "visibility"; Liberals see them as people in need. Conservatives see them as potential troublemakers. Politicians, news people, opinion leaders, all are concerned by the difficulties lived or created by immigrants. Those immigrants, or visible offspring of immigrants, who have accessed the "elite", become privileged interlocutors.

So, any possible dialogue between the immigrated community and the original nation tends to be organised within this mixed "élite", and drift away from... well, the **plebe**. This, I am afraid, might be particularly true when the "élite" is structured by centuries-old affinities, solidarities, old-school-ties and back-scratching traditions.

This "élite" gets wrapped up in itself, and deals with issues in abstract terms, to achieve or to bolster positions of power in the political game. It tends to drift away from grassroots reality. They focus on "integration", "assimilation", "rejection", "discrimination", "racism", "xenophobia", "Islamophobia"... forgetting that **people** are concerned.

Britain, once the greatest industrial power in the world, has seen factories close one after another. Not because of EU, but because of the decision, by British rulers, that finance was the future of Britain. That it was a wise decision may be questioned, as the City is now losing her pre-eminence - to New York. The power of Britain rested on its working class, these millions of factory workers, who in wartime were the best soldiers in the world.

As they lost their jobs, these men and women have seen newcomers take new jobs. They have been hearing citified gents explaining that "immigrants stole the jobs" or reversely that "immigration had no effect on jobs". They just saw that they had no job, and that money was getting scarce. Now they react with their instinct. They are the foot soldiers of resistance against changing times. And everything has been done, for decades, to make them stay on the losing side.

Because they are "plebs".... They have been invisible for a long time

What the f**k! A Government's duty is to its citizens. In changing times, a Government must act to make its citizens capable of adapting to new conditions. These new conditions include immigration. And cultural clashes. And racial and religious misunderstandings. The first duty of a Government is to apply the law of the land with equity to all who live upon the land. The second duty is to reassure all those who feel endangered, that somebody cares for them.

I hardly see that. What I see is politicians. Smart and slick look-alike **Toffs**. Poll-minded electoralists. People attracted to those very Nazi or fascist rules that Britain has fought ALONE.

Bland city gents or Musical comedy squires in cashmere coats swigging beer in posh refurbished pubs, trying with a commercial traveller's grin to persuade voters that they will change everything.

 I see old school ties tut-tutting about the bad manners of the **plebe** and calling "scum" honest working class people whom nobody has bothered to help living through the years of change.

I have been a boy in post-war England. I know how much respect must be given to the working class that has made the prosperity of Britain and its victory in War.

This is why, should time permit, I would gladly join a demonstration of the English Defence League. Not to show adhesion, but to show respect and understanding. And should they find my sympathy unwelcome, they will have a perfect right to kick me out.

45

WHAT IS IN ISLAM?

4th May

I do not give a fuck about what is IN Islam, or IN any sort of religion whatsoever. That's the business of religious people. I am not religious. I believe in God, I respect all the Prophets - all their names be hallowed - as inspired by God **in their time.** I see no reason to follow the norms and dogmas built up after them along centuries by people who certainly were learned and good people, but to whom I have no obligation.

Since I have undertaken this blog, to raise my unimportant voice in the debate about Islam, Islamism, the United Kingdom and Britishness, I have been deafened by two rather loud types of noises. One is the daily exchange of invective, insult, and threats, between extremist camps, using arguments full of passion, but devoid of any reason. I shall address this issue later. The other noise comes from the grave mumbling of pundits pretending to make sense of the senseless hatred that threatens to destroy much peace and many peaceful lives.

These learned people do a flourishing business in fishing out quotations from books held to be sacred, in order to support a **political** issue. They may spew fire and sulphur to send innocent fools get themselves killed and kill other innocents. They may produce dark threats from under the dust of centuries to demonstrate that no good may ever come from one camp or another. They may, from under the same dust, produce honeyed words of peace and love that readers of History may point out as blatant lies.

All the books of the Bible, the Quran, (respected names both) plus all the additions and comments that have been made by the Fathers of the Church, the Learned Rabbis, and the Caliphs and Muftis and Ulema and Mullahs that have flourished like the green bay tree under the shade of religion, all this constitutes an awesome corpus of theological literature, into which all theologians wade happily.

Now theologians have been put on this Earth by the Lord Almighty only to the purpose of having discussions on theological issues, creating thus new issues that will breed more discussions. They have no more reason to establish consensual truths than a thirsty man to pray for drought.

By which I mean that those who wish for peace on Earth - and particularly for peace between Muslims and Non-Muslims in one of those peace-loving spots of Earth that are our countries, must expect nothing from the confrontation of religious and learned pundits. On the contraries, war mongers on all sides will always find, in those sessions of clever discussion, something to kindle the fire of violence.

The contents of any religion is important only for those who adhere to it. Theirs to interpret according to their conscience and, if possible, quietly.

The law of the state is the product of centuries of national culture. In our countries, it has the unique privilege of having been established through democratic process. I believe it has, thus, pre-eminence over the various faiths, creeds, philosophies, doctrines, customs, inclinations, and tastes of a population that grows more and more diverse in the freedom of its lifestyles.

It is certainly not an expression of hate for any community than to demand that it comply with the law of the realm. It is certainly not oppression of any community than to demand that its members refrain for public offences to the symbols of the country, to its administration, to its Armed Forces.

As Dr Rowan Williams brilliantly expressed, Britain (and that goes for other European countries) has got to the Post-Christian phase. That means for me that **all** religious doctrine falls into the sphere of individual choice, and can no more interfere with civil life. Some may call this secularisation. Words do not matter.

The law of the land is passed by Parliament, implemented by Government and Administration. It does not have to be bent for the convenience of any creed.

Everyone in the land must submit to it - or pay the price - or move away. Keep religion - and atheism - a private matter.

This is why I say, with all due respect, that I don't give a hoot about what is and what is not, in Islam or any religion whatsoever.

46

ISLAMOPHOBIA IS RACISM

5th May

It is true that some hypocrisy helps people to live together - but when real difficulty arises, truth is an almost surgical necessity. Tense relationships between communities are a problem that cannot be solved with lies - albeit this be the favourite method of politicians of all colours, who prefer to push the issue aside, for their successors to deal with it.

One lie that will not help solving the "Islamic/Islamophobic" crisis in England is the pious denegation of racism: "I am not a racist: I oppose Islam which is not a race but a religion"... Shame! Hate and discrimination are equally bad if they apply to race, colour, religion, origin or sexual preference. Call it Xenophobia - the hate of whatever is strange or foreign. So our pious Islamophobic citizen is just a bigoted racist. Period.

We are dealing with people who reject entire communities on the sole ground of their foreignness - and they build up arguments with the same sort of fibs and slander that has been used for centuries whenever outsiders were used as scapegoats by unscrupulous politicians and dictators to distract the attention of the people from real issues that were not addressed, out of incompetence or corruption.

One of these mythic arguments is about the outsiders being cruel to children. That was used against the Christians two thousand years ago, then against the Jews more recently. I am not sure some accusations of that kind were not whispered between Catholics and Protestants in the now virtuously forgotten times of our religious wars. Now let us be clear about this: no race, no religion, nothing can excuse certain crimes, and the law has to deal with the criminals equally and fairly, whatever their personal status. But this does not give anyone any right to tax an entire population with the offences of some of its members.

It is well known that a significant number of English and other European travellers have been practising "sexual tourism" - ever since travelling has become trendy and easy. In a 1978 cult film based on Agatha Christie's Death on the Nile, starring Peter Ustinov, Bette Davis, David Niven, Mia Farrow, Angela Lansbury and more... there is a scene of scores of small Egyptian boys "mooning" at the passengers of the Nile cruise boat. I have no doubt this scene was judged hilarious at the time. I still find it very funny. Still, it is a bare-...faced evocation of a paedophilic market - where the buyers, i.e. the criminals in our present frame of mind, were "white", that is, English and Europeans. There have been scandals of that nature recently, in North Africa and in Asia; sometimes the guilty party has been tried accordingly with the law of the country of his crime - and well done! But nobody has ever suggested that the British, or the French, were all child-abusers and paedophiles.

Crime is individual. There can be no collective sanction. Slogans based on generalisation must be banned, as both expressing and provoking hatred. As I said before, it is legitimate to be angry at a crime and demand punishment of the guilty - but it cannot be permitted to hate innocent people.

Of course, the opposite is true, and the hallucinated bearded preacher who calls on murder against all those who do not abide with his faith cannot be permitted to spread his own hate. The law should fall on him with its utmost severity, whatever his popularity with the press.

47

THE WAR IS ON

7th May

Obscure, evil ideologies want to deprive the European man, not necessarily of his material possessions, but essentially of this freedom of choice. These ideologies are embedded in the "holier than thou" prejudice that one group "knows better" or "is better" than the rest, in theories of racial or religious supremacy that we cannot accept.

We have painfully survived the attacks of Nazism and communism. Do we remember them?

We have been warned by Huxley, Orwell or Burgess about the ever-returning risk of totalitarianism. Did we heed those warnings?

Nostalgia of the Nazis and of communism still roams across Europe. The tragedies of Hitler and Stalin are probably fresh enough in our minds, that only small groups carry these loathsome messages.

They may become more dangerous as our countries become more vulnerable, in a global economic and geostrategic system that lacks stability and offers little prospect of bettering for the material situation of the world population.

But the most immediate danger lies in an ideology that combines the most extreme religious supremacism with an apparent benignity of purpose, an ideology supported by the vindictive anger of nations that had chosen to stay away from the current of civilisation, and accuse us of having taken advantage of their own folly and backwardness, an ideology developed by highly intelligent intellectuals, who have learnt all our tricks from ourselves, and now want to use them against us.

This enemy has a great strength of proselytism; it is supported by rich and ruthless states, some of them owing their power to our own lack of vision; it perverts the use of our freedom of opinion and speech to openly attacks our nations and institutions; it uses the greed of our corporations, administrations and organisations to get leverage on our economies; it corrupts our media of information; it shows the most ruthless violence and cruelty in physical actions; it uses cleverly the alternative of terror and persuasion.

Terrorising the moderate Muslim crowds, subdued by

centuries of fatalism, this enemy is **Political Islamism,** which want to impose religious supremacy, a medieval moral code, and a totalitarian organisation of the state, with total control of our actions, expressions, and even thoughts.

THIS IS THE WAR WE MUST FIGHT

48

TAKING SIDES

8th May

When I was a boy, after WWII, when Muslim Morocco justly struggled to be rid of French protectorate, we were called "Europeans" indistinctly of our real nationality. This has marked me. As a soldier I have served my country as I could. As a man I have retained respect and sympathy for North Africa, where many cultures have cross-bred into an original civilisation. I have met many Muslims - agreed with them that there was only One God, with a general message of peace and respect of fellow-men, and that theological discussions were not essential to everyday life.

As a citizen, however - a concerned observer of history and politics, I have always been, and always shall be, a "EUROPEAN".

Now that I see Europe (both insular and continental) under attack by Political Islamism - that most dangerous avatar of totalitarianism, after Nazism and Communism - I have no doubt about which side I am fighting on.

There may be differences in the perception of tactics and even strategy - but there is only one war, and one enemy. Political Islamism, a totalitarian doctrine similar to Nazism. Political Islamism uses the inertia and solidarity of a Muslim world that, however diverse in languages, history, and practical culture, is bound by centuries of fatalist acceptance and submission. Upon this Muslim world, Political Islamism exerts a considerable pressure, by terror and extortion, comparable to that of a Mafia - at a larger scale and with means much more terrifying.

I believe that the best way to fight Political Islamism is to cut it from its base of acceptance, and show the Muslims among us that they have nought to fear from the bearded bullies that use our soapboxes to call at arms against us.

I believe this view to be shared by many, and I have understood it in the last positions taken by Tommy Robinson before he was forced into temporary retirement for reasons legally unrelated to his political stance.

I understand that a move of anger has sprung, at Tommy Robinson's call, when British Troops returning from battle were insulted on English ground. I support this a soldier - with the solidarity of soldiers over the world, and particularly inside our century-old alliance that survived two World Wars, the Suez Canal affair, and lives up to the present war against terror.

I understand that the English Defence League has severed all connection with any movement linked to Nazi nostalgia and fights only for one goal: defending England and English freedom against the totalitarian threat.

I understand that they operate on public sensitiveness, denouncing globally Islam and Political Islamism. I am not sure this is the best tactics. But I am yet to see other tactics been implemented with courage and tenacity.

I understand their action is seen as a perturbation of public order, that they inscribe into a certain tradition of roughness that some polite souls deem offensive. I respect public order - up to a point. I don't give a fuck for politeness.

I believe these working-class people, both materially and intellectually abandoned and disowned by the establishment, deserve more respect and attention. Even if their very physical perception of the threat - and reaction to it - is, in my way, mistaken, ineffective, and counterproductive because it give an excuse to Political Islamism militants for bullying their own people, I think they are certainly not receiving all the attention and respect they deserve.

I perceive them as soldiers, and I think Kipling's

poem of "Tommy Atkins" applies well to them: EDL this and EDL that, unwelcome in the world of political shows where obvious mountebanks like Nigel Farage and Anjem Choudhary are center-stage, but valuable when the drums begin to roll. – And the drums are rolling now.

I am a foreigner - worse! A Frenchman! So it is quite possible that some be surprised or even offended that I should express my thoughts about British patriotism and the Muslims in Britain. I feel concerned because as a WWII boy, I admire Churchill and the fighting spirit he inspired to this great country. I feel concerned because I was a schoolboy in post-war England; because I remember the smell of coke-fires. I believe that I owe it to myself, as an old soldier, before fading away, to recognise that there is a war on and show my solidarity to those who fight it.

49

EDL THIS AND EDL THAT

14th May

Most of my friends have doubted my sanity when I announced my curiosity for the English Defence League and my sympathy for some of its members. All those who have known me some time know that I am tolerant, inclining towards liberal, not conservative values, and deeply European. I believe in God creator of the world, who has spoken through ALL prophets, repeating ceaselessly the same message to Mankind: *Thou shalt not kill,* and *Love thy neighbour.* I do not follow the rites of any religion, but I respect intensely those who do. I have many Muslim friends whom I value particularly.

And here was I going on with EDL...

EDL is a gathering of some hundreds - perhaps some thousands in all England - of men who express very strongly their opposition to anything that appears to break English identity. They are very loud against Islam, using words like sharia and halal without having any idea of what they mean really, and very angrily consider that all Muslims in the world are responsible for all the criminal offences that some Muslims commit in England.

They are not neo-Nazis, they are pure English, using urban tactics learnt from the very English tradition of rowdy support of football teams. They are Churchillian patriots. As a soldier myself, I respect patriotism, although it be a bad word nowadays in educated circles, and I do not confuse it with nationalism or xenophobia,

I support - as a man - their youthful founder, "Tommy Robinson", who has appeared to distance himself from violence and procure understanding with English Muslim organisations. When he be free again to express his views and set his course, I shall be very interested in what he does.

Meanwhile, I have blogged a few ideas, and kept up a friendly contact with men in EDL; in fact, I am rather proud of the friendship that binds me to a few of them, and I affirm solemnly that, as men of conviction and action, they are to be respected, and not despised and discarded by the "educated" classes of political commentators.

EDL springs from the depth of that English working

class that has been destroyed by successive governmental actions, starting with the infamous Baroness Thatcher. The priority given to capital, to banking and management activities, over industry, has left on dry sand a class of workers that were the pride of English industry - and in wartime the pride of English fighting forces.

At the same time - the normal flow of immigration has brought young men, with different motivations, who had access to new jobs in trade or technology. The unemployed English were not prepared to cope with that challenge.

Then, under the pressure of the American "ally", Britain has been drawn into Middle Eastern wars that were not of vital interest to her, but who touched precisely those countries where many immigrants had their roots - and families.

This makes it understandable why there is palpable tension between elements of the Muslim community in England, and the population from which springs EDL.

Something has to be done, and now. And no one can do it but the English Government. Not by spending thousands of pounds in policing EDL demonstrations, but by an effort of information, AND economic action.

There is evidence of a double injustice: Injustice against the Muslim community that should be protected from their bullies, and never confused with any party of activists or criminals. Injustice against part of the English working class, a small disadvantaged minority that must be protected from the effects of social changes that they do not understand, and resent as threats. Both injustices must be addressed equally.

Islam is a great religion of peace, which some politically-oriented preachers want to turn into a totalitarian and religious system of government, totally unsuitable and undesirable in our countries. We have not reached, in the words of Dr Rowan Williams, "post-Christianity", to regress to any other form of theocracy. We have learnt, with time, to reach individual freedom of choice, and we shall fight to retain it.

The Muslims who have made the effort to come to our countries haven't come, for the most of them, to establish their laws on our soil: they have come to work with us, to share our institutions and style of life, retaining of their traditions what can be accepted under the law of the realm. They must be protected and made welcome.

They must be respected. All communities, all minorities must be respected by a state that must arbitrate between tensions and dissensions. So must be respected every citizen or resident of Great Britain. Including those who express anger at events they believe unacceptable.

Men who have chosen to join the English Defence League is to be respected, as well as those who have decided to leave it. The EDL are not "scum", they are not "hooligans" and they are not "thugs". Yes they drink large quantities of beer and cider. Yes some of them pack a powerful punch and are Olympic-class table-throwers. So what? They are Englishmen, they defend their flag which they mistakenly believe to be in danger. They are entitled to be protected in turn.

They require attention, not suspicion, work and education, not derision. Respect always must go both ways: top to bottom and bottom to top. But it starts from the top.

.

CONCLUSION

A blog cannot go on indefinitely. When I read again
the articles that I have posted from the beginning, I
realise that I might endlessly harp around the same
facts and ideas, not getting any wider audience nor,
perhaps, being more convincing. The time has come
to recapitulate what has been said, and launch this
book, as the sum of my reflection on the anger of
English patriots confronted to political Islamism.
Anger, like fever, is the sign of a disease or
dysfunction of the public body. Like fever, it may
have healthy effects, if the cause of the disorder be
correctly addressed. If not, it may fester into hate and
seriously endanger the health and life of a nation.

Treatment of social disorder is for the politicians to
propose, for the citizens to choose and for all to
apply. Now the greenest student of medicine will
know that diagnosis is the key to cure. Political
science is not more exact than medicine, and

consequently the attempt to cure social trouble must rest on a serious investigation on the nature and cause of the trouble. As in medicine, many theories can be applied, using different methods of analysis, the goal being always to come as near as possible to the truth.

Most human quarrels arise from ignorance. Of course it is not the people's fault if they are ignorant. The ever-widening scope of education has always its blind spots. The press, radio and television have their way of distorting perspective to make it more spectacular. The social networks amplify the shriller sounds to make the music almost inaudible. It is not important to pin the fault on some community or other. What is important is to forage through the mass of information available, and get – if not to THE truth, at least to a piece of truth that may contribute to the diagnosis and therapy of the social body.

The most diverse and often preposterous things are said about Islam. It should be very clear that, although we may and must be at peace with Islam, Political Islamism is at war with us, a threat to our European way of life, and most important, to our civilisation founded on freedom of choice. What is important to us is to see the difference between Islam – a religion, and Political Islamism – an ideology.

Islam is not a cult of hate, vowing destruction of Jews and Christians.

Christianophobia and Hebraicophobia are not essential to Islam. Far from it. Jews and Christians are "the other people of the Book" – as opposed to heathen and atheists. In many countries ruled by Islam, there have been, in History, conflicts between the population and the Jewish or Christian communities. They have not been more frequent, or more brutal, than the persecutions of Jews in Christian countries. It was Queen Isabella, not the Muslim kings before her, who expelled the Jews from Spain – when they could not be forcibly converted. In Morocco, the Sultan was ever the protector of the Jews and Christians, who found refuge within the walls of his Palace in case of uprising.

Far from being a "heathen", "pagan", "idolatrous" cult, Islam has fought from the beginning against idolatry and paganism. In fact, it came up in reaction to what could be perceived as a drift of Christianity towards idolatry. Like Christianity, it has not been able to eradicate all superstition from the populations it has won over. Some fundamentalist sects, from time to time, feel anger and resentment at what they perceive as a betrayal of the Word. This has led, for instance, to the destruction of the Afghan Buddha's and Timbuctoo shrines. In the same way did the Iconoclasts first, then the Reformation, destroy images in Christian temples. The wise, however, tolerate remains of the past and weaknesses of the human soul, as long as there is no pretence at any material representation of God.

God in Islam is one, though his names are many – he is all things and the opposite. As the Christians call him The Beginning and the End, Alpha and Omega. God cannot be known, nor rightly named, nor figured by an image. It stands to reason that this definition applies to God also in Judaism and Christianity, although in different languages and with subtle variations of words. Visions of God may differ, but God is one. This is what I have tried to express by my poem "The Hill".

As Jesus said "I came not to change the Law, but to fulfil it", Muhammad is presented as the last (or latest) of the long line of prophets. Islam recognises Jesus as a major prophet, in the line of Musa (Moses). That he was born from a Virgin is also stated in the Quran. They do not, however, accept his divine nature and filiation. Christians and Jews are seen as having strayed from the original message. In fact, the Decalogue.

Theologians may argue about those fine points. We are talking about people, not articles of theology. People who live, work and love, side by side. People who try to follow the same rules as they have been taught to them in different perspectives. Islam, as a religion, needed by some people to manage their connection with the Unknown and to govern their personal or family morality, is certainly nothing to distrust or fear in our societies, built upon Greco-Roman foundations, and Judeo-Christian tradition, now evolving into post-religious humanism.

Islam, as a religion, is not an obstacle to Muslims living in peaceful harmony within our European communities (both insular and continental). Now Political Islamism, as an aggressive, conquering and totalitarian ideology, is quite another matter.

Religion is a means for human communities to organise their relationship to the Unknown and the incomprehensible. Call this God for communication's purposes. It serves as a base for public morality and the rules of law organising relationships within the community and outside it. As "political" means "touching matters common to the city – or people", religion evolves naturally into political doctrine. This was ever so. From the Roman Emperors who called themselves gods, to the Tudor wars, when the sibling Queens identified themselves to the Roman creed or to the Reformation, to Islam to-day, in countries as different in culture and origin as Iran and Saudi Arabia, sharing an identical and frightening interpretation of religious law.

Political doctrine based on religion, or religion used as a political doctrine, always tends to totalitarianism. This is one of the constant factors of the human social mind. One wants to force happiness upon the others – or kill them. Thus were Roman Emperors deified and adored in the hills of Morocco as in the forests of Germany or in the streets of Rome. Thus did the Christian priest preach conversion to any Infidels as had been spared by the European soldier. Thus goes the Western missionary of to-day peddling democracy and asserting his domination on economy. Thus goes Political Islamism, nowadays the growing force of totalitarian imperialism, and a danger to us all.

Political Islamism is not just about mad preachers shouting their gibberish of hatred from imam's pulpits or from Hyde Park Corner soapboxes. It is a doctrine to take over the world, very clear, very precise, very elaborate, and very scary. Certainly it was always latent in the Islamic world, but one might say it has really sprung from the violent confrontation of Islamic populations with European imperialism.

Islam, a brilliant and largely dominant civilisation around the Mediterranean when mediaeval Europe painfully emerged from the darkness of post-Roman Barbary, was rolled back at the Renascence and did not share nor endorse the scientific changes that led to the industrialisation and expansion of our countries. As British, French, German industrialists lobbied their governments for more natural resources and cheaper manpower to feed capitalism, the Ottoman Empire – last avatar of the great Caliphates of yore – and the Moroccan Empire – last heir to the intercontinental dream of *Al'Andalus* – were easily deprived of their independence, freedom and dignity.

After two world wars and the fall of the 19th Century colonial empires, it was natural that some minds considered that a pendulum of History was swinging back, and there is no doubt that post-colonial revenge is an element of Political Islamism. The main colonial powers, the U.K. and France being together on the front line.

Christianity and Islam share the same vision of planetary Salvation by the Word and Law given to all by divine intervention, implemented by a certain code of morals and rites. Communism has the same global approach, minus God, plus Marxist analysis of economics. Judaism and Nazism share a strong vision of a supremacy based on race or/and religion. The thinkers of Political Islamism have benefitted from the advantage of coming last.

They apparently impose a very basic creed, simply summed up by few words, and that does not collide openly with other creeds, so that catechisation is made easy. The colonial revenge element is always in the background, so that it seems natural for them to pose as a "religion of the poor" – when the Christian churches are wide open to criticism on this particular point. If one adds the seduction of the unknown, the attraction of the young for adventure, and a certain taste for the exotic, one can see why Islam may be attractive, here and now, as the religion of Peace it is – in its way.

Political Islamists capitalise on that force of attraction, but it may well be that any war is better than the peace they propose to establish. Because their ideology is based on determinism and subservience, while we are guided by freedom of choice, and, in the words of W.H. Auden, honour the vertical man, not the horizontal one.

To get a clear picture of Political Islamism, one might read "the Time of the Bedouin", by Ian Dallas. The first part of the book, in the **perspective of Nietzsche, is an absolutely remarkable analysis of the history of Europe since the end of the Middle Ages, pointing to the domination of capitalism and the hegemony of the Banker. Then the author turns to prospective political thoughts, announcing the brave new world of** universal *sharia*.

Another book gives an even clearer picture of the future designed for us by Political Islamists. The author, Sayyid Qutb, was a member of the Muslim Brotherhood, sentenced to death and executed in Egypt in 1966. His book "Milestones" is an extremely clever methodology, written with the simplest and most effective words, of implementing Islam as a universal rule, replacing all other laws with the law of Muhammad – as read by clerics along fourteen centuries. This book might be as significant of the dangers of our times as Hitler's "Mein Kampf" has been for the 1930's.

Political Islamists are the closest thing we can find to Nazism nowadays.

They are supremacists and totalitarians: everything must be governed by their one religious ideology, and enemies, dissenters, and misfits must be destroyed. It is startling that, although Muslim travellers and calculators have given to the world the essential tools of circumnavigation and mathematics (the compass and the zero digit) the Political Islamists refuse all the progress that has been made in the knowledge of the world. This, I expect, will bring on their eventual failure, because reality always triumphs over ideology.

Meanwhile...

Meanwhile they thrive and flourish like the green bay tree.

The threat of Political Islam is a fact, as it is fact that Islam in itself is the religion of millions of people who have no wish for the kind of presbyterocracy (or dictatorship of the priests) that the Muslim Brotherhood and like groups want to establish.

It stands to reason that if people and families have taken the extraordinary step of emigrating, at the cost of much sacrifice, even to risk death, it is because they aspire for a different existence – a better one; because they want to enjoy for themselves and their children the style of life that they believe to be that of England, or France, or any of the countries to which they migrate. That style of life means material comfort, work, health and care, benefits, but, most important, it means freedom, freedom of movement, freedom of trade, freedom of thought, freedom of speech, freedom of religion, all these beautiful words that we in Europe are so loud and proud about having given to the world.

Why should immigrants turn away from their goal and set to destroy the very country into which they aspire to live? It does not make sense. Of course there is the old theory of a world conspiracy, of hate and greed moving outsiders to replace insiders... This morbid fantasy, a good resource for the writer of fiction, does not rest upon any other ground than the deep fear of some unknown Devil at work, and, basically, Man shying away from responsibility and refusing a realistic analysis of History.

Over-simplification however, together with that animal distrust of any difference, leads people to confuse individuals or groups with a larger community. There was an old joke of a French traveller spending one night in Dover and writing home: "British women have red hair" because the landlady happened to have a head of that flaming colour. Well, the obvious stupidity of this Frenchman is plainly reproduced by all those people who attack "Islam" whenever a crime is committed by a person of that religion, and indict a whole population for the offence of some individuals.

Such confusion is extremely dangerous, because "good" Muslims do not see any more the point of being "good" if they are pointed out as "bad". Migrants, a little bewildered by their new surroundings, suddenly fearful of difficulties they had not foreseen and might not override, tend to flock together. This is true of rich expats in sunny countries. This is even truer of simple immigrants in dusky lands. The Political Islamist is at home in the Muslim community. He knows all the codes, he shares the language and the collective memory and he may even be family. Is it not natural that his fellow—immigrants turn to him for protection when they feel the world around them become hostile?

The Political Islamist is ever too ready to give advice and protection. Just as the benevolent Godfather from the Sicilian *Famiglia* is willing to give protection and advice to the immigrant from Palermo or Catania... Protection, but at a price. We know well that scheme, popularised by so many books, films, and TV series. It is a survival of the old feudal spirit of Europe, in which the stronger man forced the weaker to work and fight for it. It is called the *Mafioso* system.

If we do not want the Political Islamists to destroy everything we enjoy, everything our forefathers and ourselves have fought for, we are committed to fight a Mafioso network, using Mafia rules to force a community to help and serve a bunch of Nazi-like activists. I call them the Islamafia – although, just like the old Mafia or Cosa Nostra, it may be divided into embattled factions. They are a mafia. They want to control the world. They dominate and bully their own people, to extort funds, to recruit henchmen, to fade themselves in the benign shade of "mutual support".

Whenever we associate crime, committed by a Muslim, with the entire Muslim community, what we do is to push the innocent under the protection of the guilty, to strengthen the hold the political militants have upon the ordinary believers. This is exactly the contrary of what should be done: the Muslim community must be helped to be rid of her bullies, more or less heavily bearded, harsh- or soft- spoken, whose motive is to gain momentum in their attack of our world.

In the same way that the Nazis in Germany gained slowly momentum from the 20's to 1934, then became a force too strong for most Germans to fight, Political Islamism is now gaining momentum. I believe it is still time to stop it, and prevent the innocent Muslims from total indoctrination. If you think that it is not important, ask yourself if it would not have been important to stop the progression of the Nazi party in Germany before it started eliminating Jews, Gypsies, Homosexuals, and finally triggered the Second World War.

Because it is the very same scheme we see reproduced before us, a ruthless supremacism based this time on religion not race, but with the same vision of a totalitarian world, from which all "deviants" or "dissenters" or "misfits" would be mercilessly destroyed. Again, the Jews, the Gypsies, the Homosexuals are on the front line – but they would never be alone.

IT HAS HAPPENED BEFORE: it is well known that the Grand Mufti of Jerusalem and Adolf Hitler had a great regard for each other, and that thousands of Muslims were lured into the *Waffen SS* to fight for the Reich. Now this – again – must not lead to confusion: thousands of other nationals were also lured into the German Army and that does not reflect upon their countries. As for the Grand Mufti, it would be a very European mistake to see him as some sort of Muslim Pope, giving out orders to be carried out in the smallest mosque. He was just this: a Political Islamist who had achieved a position of clerical pre-eminence.

Political Islamism must be fought, and it can only be fought by separating it from the Muslim crowds that it manipulates and terrorises. And to do this, what we must do is show respect to the people who make up these vulnerable crowds, both terrifying and terrified.

Respect is probably the keyword of human relationship. For a long time, people have wanted to be respectable. Now they want to be respected and this is not just wordplay. Respectable is conforming to standards to be accepted, respected is being accepted however different from standards. From one status to the other, our society has gone a long way, and even in our global village, we must accept that all communities have not moved at the same pace. Respectability is appearance, respect is a rule for mutual understanding

Respect is no one-way relationship. It goes many ways, and as our society becomes more sophisticated and more complicated, so does respect take many forms, weaving an intricate network of mutual regard. The sort of respect that comes to mind immediately, from underdog to top-dog, is not respect – it is fear. If a 15 stones, 7 ft. tall man shows me his clenched fist, I shall reasonably fear him – If he smiles and extends an open hand, I shall respect him, certainly for his strength, but mostly for not using it, and thus respecting me, whom he could have so easily flattened.

I used to spend much of my time, in the late 1970's and early 1980's, in a beautiful old village hidden in the hills of Portugal. A medieval village with walls burst open by the armies of Napoleon, with a 14th century castle, a renaissance pillory and a granite manor house. The old men of the village used to doff their cap before the coat of arms on the manor's door. That was one form of respect. The lord of the Manor was an old gentleman of ancient nobility and great culture. Whenever he met a stranger in the village, HE doffed his cap first, as a courtesy to the unknown visitor. That was another form of respect, which I have never forgotten.

The guest, the visitor, the newcomer, deserves respect. Life is not a school yard where new boys must be properly drilled by their elders and supposed betters. A man is a man, never more, never less. This is why the stranger in a country, the immigrant, the Muslim in a country that retains the trappings of Christian culture, is entitled, from those who came before him, to have his beliefs respected, as well as his personality. I know of nothing more stupid, moronic even, than some actions against mosques that happen sometimes, as well in the U.K. as in France or other countries of continental Europe. It is cowardly, as any hit-and-run attack against a monument. It is counter-productive because it hurts the weakest members of the community: those who need to pray and assemble in the place of cult. Precisely those whom the Political Islamist wants to recruit as bomb-fodder. In good logic, justice should prosecute the men who attack mosques as accomplices to the recruitment of terrorists.

Most of my friends will reply with indignation that the law of the land must apply to whomever is on the land, and that the newcomer, Muslim or any immigrant, must conform to it. Period.

Did I ever say anything to the contrary?

What is the purpose of the legal system of any

country? We might say it is to draw a frame in which all the citizens of that country can exert their rights, enjoy their liberties, apply their energies and be protected from each other's encroaching on those rights, liberties and applications of energy. This is basic law. It includes education, labour, trade, neighbourhood, traffic rules, etc. It can also be said that it implements the national solidarity that gives its identity to the country: wealth repartition, health, social security, common defence, and cultural ambition would come into this file.

It is somewhat evident that anyone applying for residence or citizenship, or even any visitor, must abide with the rules of the land. Some are rather simple and easy to understand. Even a French driver is quick to realise which way goes the traffic in Britain, and that, for him "right is wrong and left is right". Some get a wide publicity through the press and other media: same-sex couples are not encouraged to visit certain countries where their relationship be against the law. However, the legal system of our countries has grown very sophisticated and complex in time, for the greater satisfaction of the legal professions.

It is difficult for an immigrant to grasp at once all the rules that are routine for the indigenous population. As it is difficult for him or her to master the language of their new country. The idea that they should not be admitted if they don't qualify to a test of sorts is not a bad idea in itself: it does not fit, however, into the pattern of most migrating process. The would-be migrant, often, has no time nor opportunity to learn the language and civilisation of the country he goes to. I believe there is a percentage of migrants that would not have to migrate to Britain in the first place if they were educated enough to be fluent in English and familiar with British culture... They would have good jobs in their countries...

The answer to this is, of course, to educate the newcomer, to teach him the fundamentals of language, culture, and the legal system. This is not an imposition on immigrants, this is a duty of respect due to them. It is our duty to inform them, and clearly so, that actions that were considered of little importance in their old country become offences or crimes in the new country. Once the information has been digested, it would be a lack of respect to tolerate behaviours from them that are not tolerated from nationals.

In our countries where equal rights and equal duties are fundamental to our system of justice, it stands to reason that we have a duty to immigrants to make them understand our laws and follow them as we do. This is what I mean by respect: explain the rules first, then make no difference. The newcomers must understand the rules, but on the other hand, we must understand what difficulty they may have.

There must be a clear understanding of what is acceptable and what is not, on the principles of justice and equality that are fundamental to our legal system. Other systems may be founded differently, perhaps on religious bases. Not ours. Even if the general culture of most European countries be marked by the influence of one or other form of Christianity, most of our laws and rules issue from a secular philosophy of humanism, which springs from the double heritage of Greco-Roman civilisation and Christianity. But there it is: it is fundamental in our systems that people be treated equally, and that the State should give no privilege to anyone on account of their belonging to any particular community inside the nation. This, to me, is so obvious that I wonder at the usefulness of wording it.

When the law of the land, for instance, forbids polygamy, and as long as the lawmakers have not seen fit to change it, there is no earthly moral reason to accept it. People who have, in their own country and quite legitimately, acquired several spouses must accept that only ONE of these relationship can be given full legal status. It is up to him to decide which will be considered as concubines.

This does not affect the right of children, because there is a general tendency in our societies to accept that a child is a child, whether it be born in wedlock or not. And rightly so. Meaning that if polygamous Mr M. wants to settle in a country where polygamy is not accepted, his offspring will be taken care of – but he must decide which of the ladies stays as wife and which goes as concubine…. The importance of this, however, is bound to dwindle in time. Even in Muslim countries, the younger generations, involved in modern activities, are quite content with monogamy. This evolution is perhaps connected with greater permissiveness – and a different outlook on adultery.

Of course, crime is crime and must be punished according to the law of the land. No particular community law should be accepted touching the basic rights of any individual. Honour killing is murder. Paedophilia is a crime. Rape is rape. Whoever be the culprit – whoever the victim.

Closely related to the issue of polygamy are those of early marriage and forced marriage. We in Europe should remember that it was not such a long time ago that our young were considered nubile as soon as they reached puberty and the full usage of their genital functions. When the prospective life span of people does not reach 40, it is but natural that they should try to procreate early. We should stop looking at things through the pince-nez of Victorian spinsters. There is no doubt that, in a relatively short time, say one or two generations, the "custom" of early marriage will have disappeared in British Muslim communities. As for forced marriage, completely unacceptable because the freedom and dignity of individuals are even more important than their sexual fulfilment, it will disappear when the female and the male will have reached complete equality of rights and duties, and complete independence. This is not always the case, even in some great European nations.

Education is the keyword. A nation's authorities on Education must ensure that all the children, male and female, are taught the same principles on those fundamentals of our culture: equality of rights, freedom of thought and expression, and recusal of all discrimination. This I believe is essential. But it must never be used or perceived as a tool for the eradication of differences. Differences are natural and good. People benefit from comparing attitudes and customs.

It is an excellent thing that children at school should be informed on religions. Informed on all religions, which does not mean they may be taught any against their or their parents' will. Informing is not teaching, this must be clear. In this I support totally those teachers who insist in taking children to churches, mosques, temples or synagogues, and explaining what takes place there, to dispel that fear of the unknown lying at the bottom of racial and religious hatred.

When both natives and immigrants make the effort of understanding each other – and it really is a great effort – it will be easier for communities to live in mutual tolerance.

For some people, tolerance is a bad word, for others it is a magic formula to be repeated endlessly as on a prayer-wheel. It is probably the most difficult principle to implement, or quality to exert. Tolerance means acceptation of what causes us a discomfort smaller than the comfort it provides to others. The difficult thing is to make an objective comparison of things entirely subjective. This is the question: What is offensive to me that is not to my neighbour? And why should I accept it?

We are here at the core of the matter of how different people relate to each other. The saying that an Englishman's house is his castle implies a complete protection of privacy. This, in fact, translates the animal's drive to protecting its territory. Everyone, as an animal, builds around oneself a sort of invisible bubble, and resents as an aggression any crossing of its virtual frontier. Senses are used as detectors of intrusion and senses react differently for different people.

Some people are offended at a stare, some react at hand contact, some wince at bass sounds or at trebles, some hate the smell of garlic.... Everyone's privacy is constantly invaded through our senses, and this all the more so as our everyday grind forces us to live in impersonal concentrations, the symbol of which may be the commuters' crowd at peak hours.

Socialisation is the way we learn to minimise aggression and reaction. Only early socialisation keeps our life from being a constant brawl. People who have dogs as pets know how important a part of training socialisation is, as a process of making the dog accept the presence, then the company of other dogs. We humans are socialised from our birth, within our families, in kindergarten, at school and lonely kids do not develop into pleasant personalities.

Socialisation is not obtained by any magisterial teaching. Any more than social tolerance can be the result of grand speeches or the making of law. Children are socialised by being together, playing together, discovering together the strange things that are in life. Now we talk about adults confronted with like problems, living similar situations, jostling each other in the everyday bustle of urban life, and realising that the same questions may not always bring up the same answers. Instead of being shocked at differences, people must accept them with curiosity, and share, yes share experiences and sentiments.

The difference in lifestyle, between a Muslim family and a non-Muslim one, is probably most conspicuous during the month of Ramadan. It is a month of fasting, not very different in its purpose of soul purification from the Christian period of Lent, however much more exacting.

A person following the rules of Ramadan may not swallow anything before daybreak and dusk. And "anything" means not a drop of water, not a whiff of smoke. This is not an easy rule to follow, particularly in a non-Muslim environment. In the hot months of Summer, the days are very long, and the thirst is exhausting. In the European Wintertime, it is the cold outside that makes it painful not to be able to warm up over a cup of coffee. As the Muslim year is shorter than ours by 11 days, all festivals – and the Ramadan "move backwards" in the year, next Ramadan coming 11 day before the current one. It may surprise that this calendar follows the lunar year, but do you know that the Jewish Passover and the Christian Easter also are set by the first Full Moon of Spring?

Ramadan is a month of sharing – the evening breakfast is important of course, and people are concerned with their neighbours. After the meal, it is not uncommon that families visit each other and get together to commune in sympathy – and partake of sweets... The month of Ramadan – and the final festival, Eid ul Fitr, are great occasions for neighbours to meet – and talk. Why not knock at Mrs Mahmood's next door with a home-made cake, sometime during Ramadan? Those small, unimportant, interactive gestures, are capital to establish confidence, and show mutual tolerance.

Of course different customs cause surprise – and may result in intolerance – on both sides. Remember our own customs have changed along the years – and rather quickly so. My own catholic grandmother never went out bareheaded; she frowned at trousered women, disapproved of my close-fitting jeans, and glared at the first mini-skirts. Yet she was neither bourgeois nor bigoted. The frantic rejection of *halal* and veiled costumes is but a thin disguise of basic xenophobia and racism, and remember: human nature reacts strongly to interdictions. The discussion about *burka* has had for obvious result that more women have chosen to wear a veil.

To live and let live is the basic rule of tolerance. Accepting difference, however, must not become some sort of counter-intolerance. A shopkeeper is perfectly entitled to sell – or not to sell – liquor or pork flesh – why not? He must make it clear to the patrons that those goods are or are not available in his shop. This is courtesy. However it is unacceptable that a sign should be put in a public place indicating that a particular law is applied in that place. I have seen photographs of posters indicating that a neighbourhood was ruled by Sharia. If those photographs are genuine, such posters are offensive and should not be tolerated. Respect, as I have said several times, goes both ways.

This indeed could be my final conclusion. Respect, not hate, is the solution.

All this has been written thinking of Tommy Robinson, who created EDL and retreated from it as he feared it might engage on a course of violence and hate that would have served no purpose, particularly not that of defending England. The hazards of life have given him an opportunity to reflect about his commitment and envision his action to come. Personally I think he has a great future. His charisma, his forwardness, and his personal appearance make him a target for the media, and a welcome guest in the arena of political shows. He is certainly a fighter, a leader of men, and an organiser of dissent, and men like him are needed in wartime.

We are indeed at war. But it is not a war against terrorism, although some put all their strength to persuade us that it is. Terrorism is nothing but warfare technics. As guerrilla warfare, it is used by the weaker and less well equipped party against the stronger party.

Terrorism is used as a weapon against our society of plenty, safety and anonymity, because it touches anonymous victims, because it disturbs our sentiment of security, because it touches us where we are most vulnerable: in the economy of communications, transport and energy. It is used by the party who has a great wealth of people ready to fight, even untrained, and to be sacrificed anonymously.

We engage it by spending billions in equipment. When we actually send men to fight, we overload them with an incredible weight of equipment, and every individual death is resented as a drama – because we care for people that we cannot afford to spare. This is the way of modern war: it has no reason to stop as long as there will be men ready to fight, and industrial forces that need a constant output for their production of sophisticated armaments.

The real war is against hunger, thirst, poverty, unemployment, disease, inequality, brutality and cruelty against women, children, and the weak.

We believe that these evils will be solved by education, liberty of thought and expression, freedom of trade and movement, individual dignity, and mutual respect. The other party believes that everything must be solved in submission to a universal rule suppressing all liberties, reducing education to catechisation, denying individual dignity and choice.

We know there are failings in our system and try to mend them; we try to take care of the casualties. The opposite party will admit of no failure, and eliminate the misfits.

That was, exactly, the position of Hitler and the Nazis. Now it is the position of Political Islamism, where the threadbare theme of racial supremacy has been replaced by the more insidious and pervasive theme of religious supremacy. But it is the same choice we have to make, between being vertical men or horizontal ones...

This is not a matter of "left" and "right" whatever those terms may mean.... Or rather, the totalitarian system that is threatening us will let no one choose between right and left. They only define right and wrong – and to be wrong means to be punished or eliminated. This is the enemy. This is the war we must fight – and win for our children.

History has never given any proof that terrorism or guerrilla warfare could be defeated by force. Napoleon retreated from Spain; the Wehrmacht never mastered Yugoslavia; France evacuated North Africa; the United States retired from Vietnam; the Soviet Union retired from Afghanistan. From Mao Zedong and the theoreticians of subversive wars, we know that the terrorist lives within the population "like fish in water".

The only strategy that works is to drain out the water. I mean, not let the terrorist networks implant themselves among innocent people, taking advantage of religious, ethnic, cultural or social bonds. We must keep in mind that the first level of terror is to bully the community within which it hides – and from which it recruits his fighters.

Every gesture, every word of assimilation of the Political Islamist activists with the Muslim community gets the community to close up their ranks and withdraw themselves into their culture, and be more ready to listen propaganda. To the contrary, very word, every gesture towards the ordinary Muslim, to express that there is no confusion in our minds, helps to loosen the grip of the activists upon the community.

It is the citizens' right to demonstrate, and be loud about attacking a wrong and defending a right, but it must be very clear that the demonstrations target the real offenders, not a whole category of people that are terrorised themselves by the mafia-like hold of activists. These demonstrations are useful, they are healthy and they are clear indications of the people's perception of what has gone wrong. Street movements like the English Defence League, as founded by Tommy Robinson, and as long as they do not drift into unacceptable forms of violence and racism, are needed to remind the politicians of the smouldering anger of classes that feel – rightly or not – that they have been left down the road.

All along this blog, I may have seemed over-critical of the intellectual and the religious – mainly because of my own recent withdrawal from religion. This must be corrected: I have no doubt that intellectual discussion is necessary to focus on the essentials. Millions of people need religious reference to give coherence to their moral life; whenever clerics endorse dialogue instead of anathema, procure common ground instead of opposite strongholds, a great step is made towards mutual understanding, and inter-faiths initiatives in Great Britain are extraordinary positive, both in number and in quality, a strong factor of hope.

These religious and philosophical encounters draw a wide frame to all actions tending to the same goal: making all religious and non-religious groups live happily and freely in the same country. It would remain an empty frame, if, at the same time, citizens did not take upon themselves to make small but determined gestures at community level, at neighbourhood level, at street level... People shopping, people picking their children at the school gate, people should all wriggle out of the corset of fear that the media are slowly imposing, and talk... then they would find out that they have much more in common than they think – and that their differences do not matter so much.

Because what matters is not religion or politics – what matters is PEOPLE. People who want to live together and be at peace together, and raise their children to work and play together – not to fear but to love each other.

28th May, 2014

CONTENTS

ABOUT THE AUTHOR

Jean Pailler, an officer in the French Army, was posted in Lisbon as Military Attaché from 1975 to 1979. A privileged witness of the Revolution, he fell in love with Portugal and Portuguese culture. He has found there a powerful source of inspiration for several of his books: Some of his works have been translated into Portuguese.

He himself has translated into French several Portuguese writers – and two plays by famous English playwright Tim Fountain.

BOOKS IN FRENCH

HISTORY:
-PORTUGAL, le printemps des Capitaines – an essay
-LA LIGNE BLEUE DES BALKANS
-CHARLES Ier Roi de Portugal - a biography
    (translated into Portuguese as CARLOS I rei de Portugal)

FICTION
-ISSA GHALIL
-LA MARGINALE – a story
-LA DUCHESSE DE LA MANCHE – a novel
-AMELIA LAREDO, une tragédie portugaise
-L'EXECUTEUR TESTAMENTAIRE -AUCUNE RENCONTRE N'EST LE FRUIT DU HASARD
-THEOPHILE MARCHELOUP, le nègre de Mozart
-APPEL A TEMOINS
-LE SALAUD EXEMPLAIRE
-ORIONDE ET LES SORTILEGES

BOOKS WRITTEN IN ENGLISH :

THE SINGAPORE CANE (fiction)
MARIA PIA: the Pretender